Stages
Understanding How You Make Your Moral Decisions

Other books by Nathaniel Lande
Mindstyles, Lifestyles
The Emotional Maintenance Manual

Stages
Understanding How You
Make Your Moral Decisions

Nathaniel Lande

Afton Slade

Published in San Francisco by

Harper & Row, Publishers
New York, Hagerstown, San Francisco, London

For Andrew, Jeff, Mark, Rick, and Sharon:
Toward a better tomorrow.

N.L. and A.S.

FIRST EDITION

Designed by Paul Quin

Library of Congress Cataloging in Publication Data

Lande, Nathaniel.
  Stages: understanding how you make your moral decisions.
  Bibliography: p. 152
  1. Ethics. 2. Moral development. I. Slade, Afton, joint author. II. Title.
BJ45.L36   170'.1'9   78-19500
ISBN 0-06-250510-6

---

79 80 81 82 83   10 9 8 7 6 5 4 3 2 1

Contents

Foreword

Sheltered behind the red brick walls of a square, slant-roofed modern fortress is the Center for Moral Education at Harvard University, directed by America's leading scholar in moral psychology, Lawrence Kohlberg. A modest, rumpled, friendly man with dark, graying hair, he is surrounded by an admiring and protective group of bright young associates and graduate students whose research he supervises. Because Kohlberg is world-renowned for his stage theory of moral development, there is a constant stream of visitors—scholars, educators, journalists, members of the Cambridge Board of Education, heads of government research projects, foundation executives—who seek his counsel. As we learned in the course of several interviews, he is invariably polite and patient and quite willing to talk freely about his work.

Across the road from the brick fortress guarding this important source of new approaches to the study and teaching of morality, stands a more traditional Harvard building with ivy-covered walls and leaded windows. Welcoming an opportunity to observe Kohlberg in action as professor of education and social psychology, we accompanied him there to a class for his graduate students. Relaxed and informal, Kohlberg darts rapidly from one subject to another, treating his students as friends and colleagues and welcoming argument. Like all great teachers, he tries to stimulate his listeners to consider, to debate, to see through their own eyes, avoiding firm stances or locked-in positions. In his classes and research projects, Kohlberg is developing a whole new breed of moral educators and sending them out to positions of influence throughout the world.

Kohlberg's graduate students and colleagues call him Larry and feel free to dissent; they also build around him a palpable atmosphere of admiration and respect. Kohlberg practices what he espouses, demonstrating that discussion and argument in a democratic setting are better teaching methods than is indoctrination. He expects his colleagues to take responsibility and to think independently.

What is this famous Kohlberg theory of stages that has taken the teaching of morality beyond the pulpit into classrooms and prisons and city streets? Kohlberg's basic concept is that all human beings go through a series of levels of moral development, each one higher than the one before, and that those stages are the same the world over, occurring in the same unvarying sequence. Not all of us reach the highest stage, but we all begin, as children, at the lowest. Kohlberg maintains that the higher stages of moral maturity do not occur until we are well into adulthood and are always preceded by mental and psychological growth, exposure to a broad spectrum of ideas and a wide range of human experience—especially of conflict.

Kohlberg's work is an extension of the pioneering research of Jean Piaget, a Swiss experimental psychologist who is an authority on the development of children's thinking. In his own studies of moral development in children and adults, Kohlberg presides over a marriage of philosophy and psychology and buttresses his theories with over twenty years of research.

The Kohlberg theory, in capsule form, is as follows:

> At Stage One, people are concerned only with simple obedience and punishment—at this level, it is the direct, physical consequences of an act that determine whether it's good or bad.
>
> Kohlberg describes Stage Two as "the morality of the marketplace." At this stage, we're primarily interested in

satisfying our own needs, but we're also beginning to learn the value of reciprocity—"You scratch my back and I'll scratch yours."

At Stage Three, we're at the "good boy, nice girl" level, at which we try to live up to the "ideal" models of behavior, the ideal being what is acceptable to our peers. Our predominant concern is to gain the approval of the group.

- Stage Four is the level of law and order. We are oriented to upholding authority and to maintaining the status quo.

The highest levels are Stages Five and Six, at which our actions and reasoning are based on principles we choose for ourselves. At Stage Five, our thinking is organized around the social contract, protecting the rights of others and fulfilling our social and legal obligations.

Stage Six is the level at which our judgment rests on universal moral principles, a rarefied plateau of thinking that enables us to view the other person's needs and our own absolutely without bias, and to base our actions on a concern for human dignity.

How did Kohlberg form this theory? He says that the origins of his thinking about morality go back to 1947, when he was twenty years old and already a veteran of wartime service in the merchant marine. That year, he volunteered to work as a crewman on one of the ships transporting illegal Jewish immigrants from Europe through the British blockade into Palestine.

The ship he served on was intercepted by the British within sight of the Palestinian coast. The crew mingled with the passengers to avoid arrest, and Kohlberg found himself interned in a refugee camp on Cyprus. Three months later, he escaped into Palestine and was present there during the war for independence.

Kohlberg found himself participating in events of major

importance, events rooted in questions of morality and justice, human rights and property rights and religious persecution. The experience raised many questions in his mind; for example, "Does the end justify the means? Is it right to use violence in a worthy cause?" All around him, Kohlberg saw his friends risking serious injury, jail, and death for their cause. Hoping to sort out some of the moral, political and philosophic issues that were troubling him, Kohlberg returned to the United States to finish college.

In those postwar years at the University of Chicago, ethical questions were considered central to a liberal education. Kohlberg's reading in his undergraduate program ranged from Aristotle to John Dewey and stimulated debates over such concepts as Kant's categorical imperative—the command of our conscience that we should act always so that what we do could acceptably be done by all, avoiding behavior that, if adopted by everyone, would render social living impossible.

Kohlberg went on to do graduate work, seeking a career that would involve him in helping people and lead to further study of the problems of morality. "I was torn between law and clinical psychology," he recalls. "But I finally settled on psychology and began a clinical project at Chicago. I read a lot of John Dewey—Dewey's ideas were very influential at Chicago in those days. And I also learned about Piaget's work. Piaget was not 'in' in psychological circles; I had to study him in philosophy courses."*

John Dewey, who had taught at the University of Chicago from 1894 to 1904, was an American pioneer in the study of how people develop morally and intellectually and how they acquire new patterns of thinking. His learning theories, widely influential in American education, were based on the idea that development takes place in stages. Dewey believed that morality grew from interaction between a developing mind and its environment. He postulated three levels of moral rea-

---

* All quotes from Kohlberg in this section are from a taped interview made in August, 1978.

soning: At the first level, we seek the satisfaction of funda-mental needs—food, glory, sexual gratification. He saw moral behavior at this level as springing purely from a need for gratification, not from any real sense of right and wrong. Dewey called this the "preconventional level." At the second or conventional level, he saw us as motivated by a need to con-form to the standards of society—wanting what the group wants, believing that what is good for the group is good for the individual. Dewey's highest level, the postconventional, is the one at which we freely choose our own beliefs and princi-ples because we perceive them as right and good. This, he suggested, is the level of conscience.

Swiss psychologist Jean Piaget, whom Kohlberg cites as the other important influence on his own ideas, has studied the minds of children for years, developing games and stories by means of which he has sought to understand how they actual-ly reason. Piaget, now 82, has explored the moral concepts of children at various levels of development and has demonstrat-ed a sharp difference between their way of thinking and adult patterns. Like Dewey, Piaget believes that moral development is not a process in which parents and teachers imprint virtues but rather is a modification of children's thinking—of how they structure concepts—as they interact with their environ-ment. Like Kohlberg, Piaget is a great admirer of Dewey and shares many of his beliefs.

Before completing his work for a doctorate in clinical psy-chology, Kohlberg interrupted his program to take an intern-ship in the psychiatric unit of a Veterans Administration hos-pital. He was appalled by much of what he saw there.

"I saw no very great concern with fairness or morality," he says. "I remember the chief psychiatrist saying one time that he'd overheard a paranoid patient criticizing him in very strong terms, and that he had ordered electroshock treatment for her. I thought that putting this patient on electroshock im-mediately after she'd complained about him was not only un-just but would hardly be regarded as fair by the patient.

"I protested. I registered a strong complaint, but I got nowhere. So at that point I decided to quit the intern program, pick up my clinical work for my thesis, and work on what I'd been reading in Piaget about the development of justice and morality in children."

Kohlberg began working with a group of 75 boys from the Chicago area, and his doctoral thesis was based on a year of interviews with them. He used nine basic moral dilemmas, considered classics in the field, inviting the boys to solve these human problems. Kohlberg studied not only what the boys said about how they would handle these situations but also the *reasoning* they used to arrive at their solutions. He probed for process and classified the replies. (One of the problems, the Heinz dilemma, asked whether a penniless man is justified in stealing drugs to save his desperately ill wife. See page 1.)

With the nine dilemmas as his instruments, Kohlberg found and correlated a variety of thinking processes, of levels of moral judgment, and, from his findings, postulated his six stages of moral development. As the study continued, he reinterviewed the original group of subjects every three years. Meanwhile he enriched his inquiry by doing research in other cultures: Great Britain, Canada, Taiwan, Mexico, and Turkey.

Twenty-three years later, Kohlberg comments on the original project: "I think the subjects have found it both painful and rewarding to have their moral views explored, their ethical temperature taken, every three years. We've had little difficulty getting the men to agree to be reinterviewed; on the contrary, they seem to like it. When we'd go back to one of the subjects, he might say, 'You know, three years ago I told you I wouldn't steal the drug. Well, now I think I would. I've been thinking about it ever since.'

"While I don't offer it as a scientific conclusion—it's more of a scientific anecdote—I believe that their being a part of the study may have steered many of these men into greater moral concern—more awareness of their own lives. Some of them have shifted from careers where there was simply a straight financial reward to more humane professions where they are involved with helping and relating to people and their problems."

The stimulus to change and grow is a natural outgrowth of the application of Kohlberg's work and that of other scientists and educators who have charted moral development. Clearly, the act of examining your own thinking, of trying to find a basis for your moral decisions, not only affects attitude but can also change behavior. It's a good demonstration of the argument that the experiment itself alters what is being observed. Certainly in the case of Kohlberg's original group of subjects, the experiment has had a growth-promoting effect, a discernible influence on the moral judgment of these men.

Morality is as much a subject of dispute among philosophers as it ever was, but Kohlberg's many years of work and study have made a profound impression in the field. His position on morality is that it represents principles for resolving conflict, and he suggests four ways of looking at it. "One view is that morality is a set of rules that tell you what to do when there's conflict," he observes. "A second is that morality is concern for the consequences of your actions when others are involved, a concern for the harm or benefit to yourself and others. A third interpretation of morality is in terms of fairness and justice—respect between people, equality and reciprocity in dealing with one another. And the fourth is that morality is the embodiment of an ideal of human personality."

At any of the stages of development described by Kohlberg, there are people who define morality in one of these four ways. "My own position," says Kohlberg, "is that fairness and justice form the central aspect of morality. That's the ground on which my work is based. That's also the ground on which, in my view, people can find a place for agreement. Many others think so as well."

Kohlberg points out that we can't really agree on the ideal

life or the ideal person. "You could be a guru or emulate a Christian saint or be a scientist," Kohlberg says. "The kind of person you are in that sense is not important, except as it enters into the area of fairness and justice. Whatever kind of person you want to be, you must still consider the rights of others."

Kohlberg believes that democracy is the best social and political form for the protection of the rights of all individuals. "However," he says, "I doubt that capitalism is the best form for getting people to recognize the rights of others. Our current capitalistic economic system doesn't promote consideration of human rights at a very high level. But, since I don't like Soviet or Chinese socialism, I don't really have a solution to offer for the ideal economic society."

Kohlberg agrees with Dewey that people reason at three basic levels, and he accepts Dewey's terms: *preconventional, conventional,* and *postconventional.* However, Kohlberg identifies two stages within each of these levels. Further, his studies are sufficiently complete and range over such a span of years in a variety of cultures that he can support his claim that the six stages are the same the world over and occur in the same unvarying sequence.

As you read further, you will acquire a clearer understanding of stage development theory and of the kind of reasoning that characterizes each stage. You'll have a better awareness, too, of your own moral assumptions and frame of reference and will have greater insight into the sources of your own behavior and that of the people who affect your life.

In this book, each stage is examined separately in a chapter of its own, starting at the beginning with Stage One, and ending at the zenith with Stage Six. As the concept unfolds, you may begin to look at your life in terms of moral stage development, and may recognize the different ways you have dealt with moral dilemmas. Throughout the book, and in a separate cluster at the end of it, you'll find a wide selection of contemporary and classical dilemmas—to consider privately or to argue out with your friends, to help you to assess your own level of moral judgment.

Suppose you've been to a dinner meeting of a committee on which you are active; your closest friend in the group is going to drive you home. You've both had a few drinks during the evening, but your friend seems fine. However, on the way, rounding a corner, he or she sideswipes a parked car and keeps right on going, over your protests. What would you do? Keep quiet? Report it to the police? Talk to your friend's spouse about it? Most important of all, what would be your reasons for your decision? Perhaps by the time you finish this book, your answer will have changed.

It is not merely interesting to examine the moral thinking that provides the frame of reference for your actions; it is advantageous, in that the act itself stimulates you to reason and act at a higher level. Looking inward—not to criticize or castigate, but to observe and analyze—brings its own reward. Somewhere deep within us all is the desire to act "rightly." You need your own approval as you progress through life. With each day come fresh challenges, and sometimes perhaps you may be dubious about your power to deal with them. And as deep as the need to act is the need to justify your actions— as child, as adolescent, as adult.

Even as we grow old, we want to look back on a life well lived. There is nothing in this book that can change the ways in which you have already acted or the effect that your actions have had. But there is much that can help you to understand the process of your past, which in turn can enlarge the possibilities of your life to come.

Acknowledgments

We wish to express our profound thanks to Dr. Lawrence Kohlberg and to his associates at the Harvard Center for Moral Education, in particular Ann Colby and Ann Higgins-Trenk, for their cooperation, time and patience, and their generous sharing of research material.

We are grateful to Jean and Richard Atcheson for the many hours they spent with the manuscript; for their valuable suggestions, their support and encouragement.

The assistance of James C. Pickett, Christopher Spurrell, Sara Madison and David Schulke in collecting the dilemmas—even to sharing some from their own experience—is much appreciated.

We thank Dr. Al Erdynast for his assistance and advice and for the helpful clarity of his work on improving the adequacy of moral reasoning.

Our gratitude goes also to Erwin Glikes and Clayton Carlson, who helped point us in the right direction; to Richard Lucas and Sarah Rush; and especially to Marie Cantlon, who kept us on the path and led us over many difficult stretches.

And lastly, our thanks to Roslyn Targ for her warm and persistent faith in the project.

Introduction

Do you sometimes wonder why you do what you do? Have you asked yourself, in moments of thought, how you came to make certain decisions that, for good or ill, led to the high and low points of your life? And when you meet hostility or deception in others, when others behave in ways that seem inexplicable, you may wonder what kind of morality—if any—animates the people who have confused or cheated or hurt you.

A concern about right and wrong is something we share with every generation back to the beginnings of civilization, and reflects an ancient question: "What is right?" While we may only rarely have to answer that question in terms of life and death issues, we do face a variety of personal dilemmas every day; every day we deal with many moral problems.

How can we understand these dilemmas and the process by which we solve them? Economist Robert Heilbroner suggests focusing attention on what people actually are, rather than what they might become. He emphasizes the limitations on our capacity for moral growth. From childhood on, Heilbroner says, we identify with larger and larger social units—first family, then neighborhood, then school, city, state, and nation. He recognizes our ability to empathize with larger and larger groups in this process. But he believes that there is a fixed limit in every culture beyond which the unifying and empathizing impulse is blocked. He thinks the world will, therefore, remain permanently divided into groups of "us" and "them."

Robert North, author of *The World That Could Be,* (1976), is a positive futurist who believes that in order to survive we must find more stable and humane ways of living and working together, and he thinks we *can*. Toward that end, as he sees it, we can learn what kind of creatures we really are, and what our potential for development may really be.

A relatively new method for pursuing that inquiry has been developed by Lawrence Kohlberg at Harvard, and that method is the subject of this book. His is an entirely cognitive approach, born of his conviction that moral development happens in orderly stages. Kohlberg observes that basic developmental stages take place with striking similarity in all cultures, notwithstanding superficial variations.

A consideration of Kohlberg's stages is a useful tool for understanding moral reasoning by observing how it differs from stage to stage. Kohlberg's theory is a new conceptualization of the details that inform individual moral decisions—yours or anybody's. It pursues the reasoning used to arrive at these decisions. It does not judge the decisions made.

You will undoubtedly recognize these stages of moral development in yourself and among your family, friends and business associates. Whole professional groups—scientists, politicians, police, criminals—can also be viewed by means of the theory of stages. It is a way to look at life, history, and literature, as if through a powerful telescope that reveals new details of familiar landscapes.

Certainly the authors of this book have been much changed in the course of our study of Kohlberg's theory of stages. We find ourselves reasoning in new ways, and so, we feel, will you. And in this recognition we find great promise—application of the theory can be highly effective in the evolution of a just society, through the development of more responsible individuals.

We came to the writing of this book for similar reasons, having to do with hard dilemmas of life and death that had greatly troubled us. I (Afton Slade) was raised in Utah, in a Mormon family. From my earliest childhood, I heard family tales of my ancestors and their flight from religious persecution.

One story has haunted me all my life, about a girl of fourteen who was with the wagon train coming west. She wandered off from a wilderness camp one morning and couldn't be found. The whole party searched for her for a full day, postponing the march. But they knew they couldn't continue much longer because they had to cross the plains before the winter storms began. Further, their supplies were limited and dwindling, and they were vulnerable to Indian attacks.

The captain of the wagon train insisted that they leave the next morning. I've always thought of how it must have been for the parents who pleaded for just one more search; equally, how intolerable for the captain to have to avoid their eyes, to refuse them, forced to put the safety of the whole group before the interests of a single lost child.

How would you have dealt with that problem if you had been the captain? What would you have done if you had been one of the parents, sitting in the wagon as it creaked forward, putting more and more miles between you and your child? Would you have wondered if you shouldn't have risked your own life, stayed behind, searched longer? But what of your other children?

Images are always in my mind when I hear moral problems discussed. I wonder how minorities can resolutely cling to their own ways in a hostile society, for example. Real people live out these abstract questions of morality and justice.

I (Nathaniel Lande) heard very similar stories when I was a child. My ancestors were Jewish, and the story of their persecution goes back thousands of years. I couldn't help but grow up with a strong concern about injustice and persecution, and I wondered why people did such things to one another.

Then I lost a friend in the Six-Day War, and that shook me. He was Paul Schutzer, a brilliant photographer. Paul's feeling for the human spirit and his compassion for people always touched me. They made his work special, lyrical. He had covered many stories, very effectively, when he was sent by *Life* Magazine to cover the Arab-Israeli Six-Day War.

As the story was told to me, Paul wanted to go out with the Israeli tanks. At first, permission was denied. But Paul reminded the officer in charge that, according to Mosaic law, "For every battle there must be two witnesses, two who are not directly involved." Paul pointed out that he and the correspondent with him would make two such witnesses. Approval finally was granted by Moshe Dayan, then minister of defense. On the evening of the second day of the war, the half-track in which Paul was riding took a direct hit.

His death, as witness to a war, confirmed my intent to be a witness for our time and prodded me toward the study of the complex moral patterns behind the thinking that leads to war and racism and injustice. I think that in pursuit of this study I have also learned something about possibilities for resolving conflict and about empathy.

I am reminded of a recent grade school class experiment that illustrates the sensitivity children can gain by walking in another's shoes. A teacher announced that the principle had determined all blue-eyed children to be superior to brown-eyed children, therefore blue-eyed children were to be given special considerations.

The classroom was rearranged so that brown-eyed children were moved to the back of the room. Blue-eyed children were given different, "special" assignments and generally given preferential treatment: longer recesses, extra dessert, more variety at play, expanded recreations and opportunities.

Every day it was emphasized how superior blue-eyed children were to brown-eyed children. There was an almost immediate change in attitudes of the children. Blue-eyed children shunned brown-eyed children, and took many opportunities to remind them of their superiority. The performance of brown-eyed children suffered as a result. Pressures were put on friendships between blue-eyed and brown-eyed children.

Some time later, the teacher announced breathlessly to the class that there had been a terrible mistake. The principal had accidently gotten the information backwards, and brown-eyed students were not inferior, in fact they were superior to blue-eyed students.

The seating arrangements were reversed, and the brown-eyed

students moved to the front of the class. But their attitudes toward the blue-eyed students were more patient and understanding. Brown-eyed students showed a willingness to help their previous counterparts, by sharing their "superior" knowledge with them.

Having understood what it was like to be treated as inferior, the brown-eyed students became more tolerant and empathetic.

A few lines we discovered recently in the newsletter of the World Plan Executive Council struck us as particularly apt for this book, and we quote it here as an observation on what Kohlberg's theory of stages can mean. "An ideal society," it says, "can never be created by telling people the importance of caring for the interests of others. A balanced life can only grow in society when every action is spontaneously able to accommodate both the interests of the individual and the interests of those around . . . The ideal society will be created by tending to our inner nature."

We feel that this book can help you in the tending.

Stage One

Obedience or Punishment
"Theirs not to reason why..."

■ **The Heinz Dilemma** What would you do if you were a man whose wife is near death with cancer, and you learn that a new drug, recently discovered by the chemist in your town, could save her? The chemist is charging $2,000 for one application of this drug—ten times what it cost him to make it. You don't have $2,000, and you go to everyone you know to borrow money. The most you can raise is only half the amount, so you tell the chemist that your wife is dying and ask him to sell you the drug for less or to let you pay the remainder later. The chemist says no. You are desperate. You break into the chemist's laboratory and steal the drug for your wife. Should you have done that? Why?

(See page 11 for a discussion of options.)

At the Stage One level of reasoning, we label what we do as good or bad according to how it is judged by others: by those in power, by those who make the rules and affix the labels, by those we try to please because they can give or withhold reward and punishment. At this level, there is no inner sense of "right" and "wrong"—we abdicate personal responsibility to play follow the leader. Stage One is primarily observed in children, rarely in adults; adults are sometimes nonplussed

1

when they realize the basis on which young children make decisions with a moral content and see how much youthful thinking differs from adult thinking. For example, Jennie, age four, informed her mother that she had been playing in the sandpile with Bobbie Hubbard and he had asked her to take off her panties.

"He said he'd give me a pear if I would," Jennie added.

"What did you do?" her mother asked.

"I told him no and came in the house."

"I'm glad you did that."

"Of course I did. You know I don't like pears."

Typically, in Stage One an action's goodness or badness is determined not in terms of its effect on someone else or its value in and of itself but in its actual physical consequences to ourselves. Jennie didn't care for the reward offered; she may also have weighed that reward carefully against the probable punishment if discovered.

Stage One reasoning sees the principles of society to be obedience to the strong by the weak and to be punishment of the weak by the strong when the strong are displeased. There is unquestioning deference to power: Al Capone once said that you can get further with kindness and a gun than you can with kindness alone. And there is a much-told story about Stalin's comment during World War II, when aides told him that the Pope was deeply concerned about some aspect of the conduct of the war. Stalin dryly replied, "How many divisions has the Pope?"

At this stage, we tend to view the social order in terms of status and to value people according to their wealth or the quantity or quality of their possessions. Rick, age nine, was telling his mother that his friend Joey's mother had to have another operation. To add to their burdens, the family had a slightly retarded younger child. Sighed Rick's mother, "I feel so sorry for Joey's parents."

Rick was shocked. "Sorry for them? How can you feel sorry for *them*? They've got two brand-new Cadillacs!"

When Davy, ten years old, is asked what he thinks are good and bad things, what makes him angry, and what makes him ashamed, he ponders for a moment.

Good things to do? Go to the store for old people, do good work at school, don't fool with the telephone, don't talk in school, don't hit other children.

Bad things? Knock over snow forts, break the fire alarm, talk in class, swear at people, stay up and see Santa Claus, hit children with sticks, make funny pictures of the teacher, spill garbage on the sidewalk.

What makes him angry? A girl called him a sissy because he ran away from a big boy; his sister got a dollar from his uncle and he didn't; he had to entertain some kids he didn't like.

What makes him ashamed? Taking a nickel away from his sister, calling her a snot, calling his uncle a big fat baboon.

What was the best thing that could happen? To become a rich boy with diamonds, rubies, emeralds, and other jewels. The worst thing he could do? To kill his dog and cat (Peck and Havighurst, 1960).

Obviously, most of these listings are items for which Davy has been either praised or punished. To him, right and wrong depends on rules set down by others, a typical Stage One orientation.

At every level of development, however, obedience is a factor deeply ingrained in us all. Our relationship to power is important not only at Stage One: As other modes of reasoning are added and we reach higher levels of moral judgment, we keep a residue of that early obeisance to authority.

In the research done with Kohlberg's original subjects, one of the dilemmas used was that of the Captain and the Troublemaker. For typical Stage One response to it, we'll use comments made by ten-year-old Mark. We'll also use Mark's later comments on this dilemma as he grows older and advances through the several stages of moral development. Mark's comments were recorded in Kohlberg's study. First the dilemma.

3

◢ **The Captain and the Troublemaker** What would you do it you were the captain of a company of U. S. Marines fighting in Korea—greatly outnumbered and in retreat before the enemy? You have made it across a bridge over a river, and most of the enemy troops are still on the other side. If somebody in your company went back to the bridge and blew it up just as the enemy troops are crossing, the enemy advance would be greatly weakened. With the head-start provided by this action, the company could probably escape. But the man who blows the bridge might not escape alive; there would be about a four-to-one chance that he'd be killed.

As captain of the company, you have to decide who should go back to do the job. You can't do it yourself; you must stay with your men and lead the retreat. Understandably, there is no response when you ask for volunteers. You must order someone to return and blow the bridge. But who? One man you consider has plenty of strength and courage, but he's a real troublemaker, always stealing from the other men and getting involved in fights. A second man who's a possibility has contracted a serious disease and is likely to die in a short time anyway, although he's still strong enough to do the job. If you as captain are going to send one of the two men, should you send the troublemaker or the sick man?

At age ten, Mark gives a typical Stage One response: "The captain's the head of the company and he can send anyone he wants. The troublemaker has to follow orders because the captain has more rank and power than he does. The troublemaker has less right to refuse because he's about the lowest man in the company."

As small children, we often felt shamed by the awesome figures who ruled our lives. Marilyn, five, wanting to dance with her playmates on a carpet of petals, pulled all the full pink heads from her father's prize peonies. She was severely reprimanded and told that the peonies wouldn't bloom again for two years. Thirty years later, the sight of peony blossoms

4

or even a reprimand from some authority figure can trigger that same flush of guilt, or remorse, the feeling she somehow should have known in advance that what she did was wrong. We all had such childhood experiences, which nudged us to greater efforts at obedience or to rebellion. If we can recall them and feel the imprint of that early stage of reasoning, which hasn't completely disappeared but is still a part of our current level of judgment, some of our present lapses into childlike behavior can be more easily understood. That level takes over when we docilely agree to something we would prefer not to do, or explode in temper over a trivial matter.

In the afterword to a new edition of *What Makes Sammy Run* (1978), author Budd Schulberg reports his shock at discovering that it is no longer an insult to be compared to his loathsome character, Sammy Glick, a ruthless, voracious little ferret who walks on the faces of all who stand in the way of his success. Glick, a symbol of self-serving opportunism, was christened "The All-American Heel" by Damon Runyon. "Now," Schulberg writes, incredulously, "self-confident young men come up to shake my hand because 'I learned so much from your book—it helped me get ahead—the more I read the more I wanted to be Sammy.'" Schulberg's analysis: "In a culture that has replaced right-or-wrong with winning-or-losing, Sammy is no longer an antihero."

In the work of Piaget, which formed the basis for Kohlberg's studies, young children in what Piaget identified as the "pre-conventional" level, ages two to six, aren't able to imagine themselves in the position of another. This is typical of Stage One thinking. Peter Scharf, in his *Moral Education* (1978), gives an example of a preschool child, Brandt, who hit another boy, Donovan, on the head. "How do you think Donovan feels?" the teacher asked.

"I dunno," said Brandt.

"How do *you* feel if you get hit with a block?" the teacher persisted.

"Donovan's crying, not me," was Brandt's response.

People who haven't reached the level where they can put themselves in another's place are incapable of empathy, of understanding another point of view. Adults who still reason at the Stage One level have exactly this limitation, the inability to see from another's perspective. Criminals often reveal this limitation with respect to their victims. Consider the case of Freddie, a 29-year-old black convicted burglar in Charlottesville, Virginia. Prior to his parole, a local organization called Offender Aid sent a volunteer to work with Freddie, to help him prepare for reentry into the community. The volunteer was Bill—middle-aged, white, a wealthy insurance broker.

Odd couple though they were, Freddie and Bill became friends. But when Freddie boasted about the jobs he had pulled, Bill, whose own home had been burglarized, said, "I really don't want to hear any more about it." He tried to let Freddie know how he felt, how other burglary and robbery victims felt. Several weeks later, Freddie wrote to Bill, "I never before thought of the people whose houses I've broken into as real people. But what you said made me understand. I've written to everyone I can remember who I've robbed, and I've apologized."

Every important decision we make has a moral as well as a practical impact. How do we reach those decisions? Are they spontaneous, or are they reasoned out? With guideposts down all around us, there's a vast concern about morals, about ethics. Who can we trust?—our doctors, our lawyers, our mechanics? Parents worry about whether their children can grow up as moral beings in a swiftly changing world.

Piaget observed that young children judge the importance of an action solely on the basis of its direct consequences. A little girl named Marie wanted to give her mother a nice surprise by cutting out a piece of sewing. But she didn't know how to use scissors properly and accidentally cut a big hole in her dress. Another child, Margaret, took her mother's scissors one day when her mother was out. Because she didn't know how to use them properly, she made a little hole in her dress. Marilene, age six, was asked which child should receive the greater punishment.

"The one who made the big hole," she replied.

"Why?"

"Because she made a big hole."

Peter, age seven, said in answer to the same question, "The second one should be punished more."

"Why?"

"Because the first one wanted to help her mother, and the second one was just playing with the scissors and she shouldn't have been."

Marilene, typical of Stage One, sees only the direct results of the little girl's actions; Peter is reasoning at Stage Two because he can see that intentions ought to be considered and that the size of the hole is not so important.

Kohlberg found that at every stage we try as best we can to determine for ourselves what's right and wrong, trying to justify our moral judgments. Even at Stage One there's already some concept of fairness and equality, an awareness of conventional moral rules—it's wrong to steal, it's wrong to lie, it's wrong to kill. But when children at Stage One are asked whether it's wrong to steal in order to save someone's life, they are torn between two conflicting rules, unable to solve the problem because they don't understand the underlying principles. They know only that what is bad is punishable, and therefore what is punishable is bad: When you follow the rules, you're praised; when you break them, dire consequences follow.

At Stage One, we see the rules set down by authority and by our own self-interest as pretty much the same. Consider the Stage One reasoning of Derek, a college student who is hosting a noisy party in his room. Despite the complaints of his neighbors, he is unwilling to do anything about the noise until one neighbor threatens convincingly that he will call the police and/or have the landlord evict him. It seems that only Derek's fear of and obedience to authority will get that party quieted down.

In the name of obedience to authority, Stage One reasoning can lead us to do almost anything. And while most typical of that stage, obedience is found at all levels of moral judgment. The famous experiment performed by Stanley Milgram at Yale University in 1963 is cited frequently as evidence of our willingness to inflict pain and threaten life. The experiment demonstrates the tendency we all have, at every age, to obey orders; thus it helps us understand behavior usually considered cruel or abnormal and shows us how strong the forces of obedience can be.

Milgram set out to test the obedience hypothesis, which holds that people will harm others when ordered to do so by an authority figure. Originally he believed that his experiment would disprove that hypothesis, and that people would refuse orders when they involved injury to someone else. Paid volunteers, college students, were told that they were participating in a learning experiment and were ordered to administer electric shocks when the subject gave a wrong answer. The shocks were to increase in intensity each time, up to 450 volts, and the volunteers were given a sample beforehand to show them how painful the shocks were.

Actually, the experiment was rigged—no real shocks were administered, but the volunteer "teachers" could hear recorded moans and cries apparently coming from the "learners". Milgram was surprised at the percentage of those who obeyed orders, all the way to administering the powerful 450 volts.

The significance of the Milgram study for the stage development theory is the fact that the Milgram volunteers were ranked on a moral maturity scale. While there is some disagreement over the rankings, results indicate that the volunteers' stage of moral judgment was significantly related to the way in which they reacted to the obedience experiment. Those at the highest levels of moral reasoning showed dramatically different behavior from those who scored at low or average levels.

Compared to the 65 percent of the whole group who kept on pushing that button, only 15 percent of those judged to be at a high moral stage continued on to the end. The major difference in attitude seemed to be that more of the high-stage people were willing to rebel, to obey their own judgment rather than the orders of the experimenters. Milgram deduces from this that it's important to have models for a constructive kind of disobedience. He believes we need more heroes like William Tell, who have the courage to defy authority when it conflicts with their own moral principles.

Obedience, so typical of Stage One reasoning, can be a complex matter. One element involved when people obey is that they are reluctant to appear rude or to embarrass themselves or a person in a position of authority. The embarrassment factor is illustrated with a dilemma that is a great favorite of comedian Shelley Berman: If you are traveling as a passenger on an airplane and happen to see flames shooting from one of the engines, what would be your reaction? According to Berman, the average person, who doesn't know whether this is a normal condition or a sign of danger, will keep silent and risk the possibility of a crash rather than raise an alarm and face the possibility of being thought a fool. This is an extreme hypothesis, but it has enough validity to make us a little uncomfortable. We have to reach a high level of moral judgment and autonomy before we become daring enough to act on our own principles rather than to save face for ourselves or for someone else.

As indicated by the Milgram study, when we can shift the responsibility from our own shoulders to those of someone else we are capable of the kind of behavior we normally condemn. "She (or he) told me to do it," has been the classic cop-out ever since Adam blamed Eve for their transgression; Eve in turn blamed the serpent.

The two requirements for growth from one moral stage to

another are mental capacity (the intelligence to comprehend higher stages of reasoning) and social experience (opportunities for role playing, for conflict, for learning a new perspective). All of a child's social experience is important—what happens in the family, the peer group, the school. If there is no warm, caring, interacting group to be a part of, the child does not acquire patterns of conventional moral thinking. We all need an environment of love, of strongly held values, in order to grow normally.

Moral development depends on the increasing ability to see, understand, and absorb reality. But if reality to a child is a nightmare of violence and abandonment, of wandering and deprivation, then that child will often reject reality and escape into a fantasy world. People growing up in a world without empathy, without positive response and positive example are unable to respond to others. Their needs are focused back on themselves, and they cling to childish ways of reasoning, seeing things in simplistic, self-serving terms.

Lee Oswald had two well-adjusted brothers. What made Lee different? "John and I had an important advantage over Lee," writes Robert Oswald (1967, p. 45). "We developed independence very early. . . . [In the boarding school] we had to. With so many children—nobody has time to make every decision for each child all the time. We had to learn to make up our own minds, to size up a given situation, decide what we were going to do about it, then do it. Sometimes we were wrong, but we knew that our mistakes were our own, not somebody else's."

Oswald's brothers had the chance to grow morally through conflict, discussion, role playing, intereaction with other children. Lee, kept close by his mother, trained to come home immediately after school and play by himself, had scant opportunity for social development. He learned to prefer a fantasy world to the real one. In his brother's words: "The violent end of his life was determined by the time he was thirteen, the effect of a thousand rejections" (p. 241).

According to stage development theory, morality is the natural product of our human tendency toward role taking or empathy, putting ourselves in someone else's shoes. It also results from our natural concern for justice, for fairness in our relations with each other, which is present even in the youngest children. At four, Lawrence Kohlberg's son became a vegetarian and refused to eat meat because, he said, "It's bad to kill animals." He had not been taught that by anyone; it was the result of the tendency of the child to project himself and his values onto other living things, other selves.

Kohlberg's studies indicate a natural sense of justice intuitively known by the child, and this personal, if childish, sense of justice was demonstrated when the son qualified his vegetarianism somewhat. "There's one kind of meat I would eat," he told his father. "Eskimo meat. It's all right to eat Eskimos because they eat animals." This was Stage One—an eye for an eye, a tooth for a tooth. His sense of values was also Stage One and didn't differentiate between human and animal life. His morality, however, was natural and internal. Moral development past Stage One builds on this tendency to take roles and on our natural conception of justice, our striving to reach a better match between our personal moral structure and the social situations we confront.

We seek to do right, and as we grow we find higher and better perspectives from which to solve the problems that develop in our lives. Our understanding expands, and gradually we begin to consider the needs and rights of others.

◤ **THE HEINZ DILEMMA—A DISCUSSION OF OPTIONS** Following are some options in response to the famous Heinz dilemma at the beginning of the chapter, and an assessment of what level of reasoning each would indicate.

Reasoning at Stage One, you would be more concerned with the physical aspects of breaking fixed rules, disobeying the law and getting punished; less concerned with your motive behind the act. Stage One reasoning would go something like this:

Heinz can't just take the law into his own hands and break into the laboratory. That makes him a criminal, and with such a valuable drug, it would be grand theft. He'd go to jail.

Concern with how much Heinz's wife means to him in a practical sense, as a companion and homemaker, would be Stage Two thinking. He would steal the drug because he *needs* his wife.

Emphasis on their relationship, on Heinz's love for his wife as well as his wanting to be a good husband, would be more typical of Stage Three. Also, some subjects at Stage Three saw this dilemma in terms of the chemist's role: As a good chemist, he should be concerned with helping people and shouldn't charge so much for the drug.

At Stage Four, the major concern again is with the law as it relates to the welfare of society—society would erupt in crime and violence if everyone were allowed to steal. No one should receive any special exemption from that law, and therefore Heinz should not steal the drug.

Stage Five is concerned with the law because it forms the basis of society's agreement to live peaceably together. By living in a society, you agree to respect and maintain its laws, and stealing is a violation of those laws. However, there's a difference between looking at a situation according to basic human rights and the legality of the matter. The chemist has a legal right to charge what he wants for the drug but is morally responsible for saving lives and making it possible for Heinz to obtain the drug.

At Stages Five and Six, human life is automatically valued more highly than property. If you have to choose between life and property, there is no question that life is more important and should always come before any alternative, even if that means disregarding the law.

Stage Two

The Morality of the Marketplace
"What's in it for me?"

◥ **The Vita-Gold Dilemma** Suppose you are James Howell, a university researcher whose discoveries may get you in trouble. It seems that the Golden Harvest Health Food Company has been funding research at the state university to test the effectiveness of various food supplements. You and your associates receive a good part of your budget from Golden Harvest.

Vita-Gold, a food supplement developed by Golden Harvest, is phenomenally successful, one of the top-selling products in its field. Foreign distributors have signed contracts for the right to manufacture and distribute it in their countries. You and your research team tested Vita-Gold before it went on the market eighteen months ago, and the result indicated a nutritionally sound and safe product.

But recently your lab has been working with a new technique, and in a routine test of Vita-Gold you and your associates have discovered that it causes a nervous disorder in laboratory mice. There is no proof that the result would be the same in humans, and it's the first negative result you've ever had with this supplement. In theory, the results of your tests are available to anyone, but in fact your reports are rarely published and are usually submitted only to the company sponsoring the research.

You know that Vita-Gold is Golden Health's most successful

and profitable product. If you bring them this disquieting news, they may cancel the funding on which your department depends. Since the product has already been so thoroughly tested, you're strongly tempted to put this new report in your bottom drawer and forget it.

What would you do if you were James Howell?

Deciding to ignore the report to protect his job and the welfare of his laboratory would be expedient Stage Two reasoning. But a concern with the possibility of the harmful effects that Vita-Gold could have on customers would indicate a Stage Five awareness of people's rights, placing the importance of human life, health and well-being above the financial interests of the lab and the Golden Harvest company.

Let's suppose that James Howell exhibits Stage Five thinking; he gives the report to Paul Drier, vice-president of Golden Harvest and the man who originally developed Vita-Gold.

What would you do it you were Paul Drier? What would you do with the report? You haven't broken any law. You've acted in good faith—your product was conceived and developed using the highest testing standards. You could ask for further tests; you could modify the product to eliminate the harmful ingredient. Or you could make the report public and recall existing supplies of Vita-Gold. Not only would this be costly, but releasing such a report would also cause tremendous repercussions in your business. It might even destroy the company. Hundreds of your employees could be thrown out of work, a disaster for them and for the town where your main plant is located. What would you do, and why?

(See page 27 for a discussion of options.)

At Stage Two, "right" means looking after one's own interests—what Kohlberg calls "the morality of the marketplace." It's moral to satisfy one's own needs; sometimes, if appropriate, it's OK to satisfy the needs of others also. Self comes first, but there's the beginning of the idea of sharing—if I do you a favor, I expect a favor in return, a simple reciprocity that has nothing to do with loyalty or gratitude or affection.

At Stage Two, people can see another's point of view and are able to take intentions into account. As at Stage One, people are still subject to rules, but now they understand that rules are not applied blindly in every situation. At Stage Two, rules can be tailored to fit the circumstances: "It's all right to break a rule if it gains some goal or advantage for yourself or someone you care about." Reciprocity—an exchange of favors—is the important difference between this level and Stage One: "You shouldn't steal because you wouldn't want someone to steal from you." One young boy even interpreted religion in Stage Two terms: "Be good to God and he'll be good to you."

People at Stage Two are still trying to be fair, just as at Stage One, but the Stage Two idea of fairness is limited to the concept that each of us should achieve his or her own ends. The basic perspective is that of separate individuals whose private needs and goals are of prime concern. From this perspective, it is very hard to reconcile conflicting interests.

At Stage Two, laws are obeyed because of the inconvenience of getting caught. People try to stay within the law to save themselves trouble. Granted, some laws are pretty stupid, but if you break them you might have to go to jail or pay a fine. The idea of challenging them because they're stupid or unfair doesn't come up.

Stage Two thinking sees no reason to sacrifice or to deprive yourself for someone else unless you can expect something in return. If a sacrifice has to be made for others, it's based on your need for them or for their services, and you expect an equal benefit in exchange.

In a typical Stage Two response to the dilemma described in the last chapter, whether the Captain should send the troublemaker on a dangerous mission, Mark, now 12, says, "The Captain could force the troublemaker to go, but it's not right because the Captain wouldn't want to do it himself. As far as right goes, a man has the right to do what he wants with his life."

Values are relative at this stage. Human life and human welfare are viewed in terms of economic worth or social usefulness. While such materialistic Stage Two reasoning is chiefly an adolescent stage, it turns up quite frequently in adults.

Consider the example of a couple who left their six-month-old son overnight with a babysitter while they went to the Rose Bowl activities. When they came home, they found a large red welt on their infant son's forehead. The sitter, a dignified, middle-aged practical nurse, quickly called their attention to the bump and explained. She said that while she had been bathing the boy a can of talcum powder had inexplicably fallen off the sink and had struck his head. She said she was sorry and added, "You can take two dollars off the bill."

The couple felt that their son's dented forehead really couldn't have a price put on it. But what a dandy Stage Two perspective for a situation—so much for a forehead, so much for a broken arm!

In his early studies, Kohlberg found this kind of Stage Two evaluation in every culture he explored. He deliberately varied his dilemmas to reflect superficial differences in each country's customs and mores, but the underlying concepts were the same. In the classic "Heinz" dilemma, shown earlier, the questions are whether Heinz should steal the drug and why. There is no "right" answer; but, remember, Kohlberg and his associates were interested in the *reasoning* behind the answer. An American Stage Two ten-year-old typically replies, "I would probably steal the drug. If he needed his wife, he should take it. It might be worth it for him to have his wife alive, even if he goes to jail." Notice that there is no mention of love, or of concern for a human life valued for its own sake.

Kohlberg had to modify his dilemmas for various cultures, and the American boy's solution is strangely apt in the case of the Taiwanese adaptation and solutions. This is how the famous Heinz dilemma was presented in Taiwan:

◤ A man and his wife had just migrated from the high mountains. They started to farm, but there was no rain and no crops grew. No one had enough food. The wife got sick, and soon she was nearly dying from starvation. There was only one grocery store in the village, and the storekeeper charged a very high price for the food he sold. The husband asked the storekeeper for some food for his wife and said he would pay for it later. The storekeeper said, "No, I won't give you any food unless you pay first." The husband went to all the people of the village to ask for food, but no one would spare him any. So in desperation he broke into the store to steal food for his wife. Should the husband have done that? Why?

Here is a Stage Two response from a Taiwanese village: "He should steal the food for his wife, because if she dies he'll have to pay for her funeral, and that costs a lot."

Or take the case of the young college student, Derek, giving that noisy party in his room. Reasoning at Stage Two, he might desist if the neighbors complain because he doesn't want them to wake him in the morning by playing their radios. This is a further instance of the importance of reciprocity at this stage.

As we progress from one stage to another, our earlier concepts remain with us. Sometimes we make our choices from that earlier orientation rather than at the higher level of judgment to which we now have access. In her book, *Changing,* Liv Ullman listens to her little girl playing and shrieking outside in the early morning. She knows that her neighbors are trying to sleep, but she lets the child play on because, as she reasons, her neighbors often play their radios and television sets loudly late at night when *she's* trying to sleep and must be up at dawn.

Even a marriage can work on this basis. Bill and Frances Asher, for instance, both have jobs; Frances is a bookkeeper, and Bill sells a line of men's clothing. He finds her a very useful wife—she keeps his books for him, he drives her to work every day. They're not particularly affectionate, they quarrel sometimes, but they meet each other's sexual, psychological, and practical needs well enough. They consider that they have a solid relationship. Their tastes and tendencies mesh: They play backgammon and tennis together, do Oriental and Indian cooking together, take turns manning the wok or measuring out the rice and curry powder. Friends have sometimes wondered what goes on between them, since they're not at all affectionate. But for the Ashers, "love" has never been a strong element in the marriage. They think of each other primarily as useful to each other, in terms of practical help supplied one to the other.

At Stage Two, with a much clearer appreciation of other people and their needs than at Stage One, we like to work together, to perform reciprocal favors and services. Sometimes this can lead to a significant exchange of goodwill as well as of material favors. It's a common practice, even in a larger context. For example, communities from different countries will pair off as "sister cities." These partnerships between two cities are usually arranged by booster organizations; they're designed to improve trade and create mutually beneficial contacts between the cities. Warmth and goodwill are undoubtedly generated, along with a contribution to international understanding. In one recent instance, after a series of severe storms in Ensenada, Mexico, its sister city of Redondo Beach, California, sent a caravan of cars, vans, and trucks down south, loaded with emergency relief supplies. A better example of Stage Two reasoning at the urban level could scarcely be found.

Vacation house exchanges stem from purely practical motives but provide both parties, as a rule, with a pleasant place to stay without costs. Often cars and beach club memberships and cleaning services go along with the deal, in a process that involves a sizable amount of mutual trust to achieve mutual benefit. This is Stage Two reasoning at the person-to-person and stranger-to-stranger level.

Consider Stage Two in the corporation-to-customer con-

18

text. During heavy winter storms in 1977-1978, the Texaco Company mailed letters to thousands of its credit card holders in Southern California, expressing regret at damage caused by floodwaters in the area and offering to extend credit to any who needed it. "Texaco's plan is dynamite public relations," said an officer in a rival company. Even though the offer had been conceived to shine up the company's image, even though the company sought to see itself described in the press as "the corporation with a heart," and even though this was a practical way to collect on accounts that might otherwise default, the gesture was no less welcome and useful to customers who were hit by a natural disaster. This was a highly sophisticated application of Stage Two thinking.

Usually, however, the larger interests of society are for the most part ignored in Stage Two reasoning, particularly if they conflict with what we see as our own self-interest. We may criticize the Victorian mill owners who intentionally discharged their effluent into the rivers used as drinking water by communities down-stream. Shocking, we say. But when antismog devices became regulation equipment in the 1960s and 1970s on cars built in this country, many people disconnected them "because they interfered with engine efficiency."

In 1966, the federal government, stimulated by the needs of the "bulge" generation of college students, offered generous loans to help them finance the rising costs of a college education. Terms were easy, and in most cases repayment didn't start until ten years after graduation. So far more than 8 million loans have been granted; almost 400,000 have not been repaid. Who are the defaulters? According to a recent survey, many have entered the ranks of the professions—they are architects, doctors, engineers, and lawyers—and they are prospering. Undoubtedly many have valid reasons for failing to repay their loans. Others justify their default with the excuse that the government hasn't made any attempt to collect from them. Reasoning at a Stage Two level, they see no direct benefit to themselves for repaying their loans now and don't consider the effect of their default on the new generation of students currently arriving at college, who find the program deteriorating and loans difficult to obtain.

Egocentric, ignore-the-rules-if-they-get-in-the-way reasoning exists also in college athletics, where the emphasis on winning and the enormous financial intestment in successful teams seems to encourage an expedient kind of reasoning. Lee Corso of the University of Indiana, member of the American Football Coaches Ethics Committee, estimates that at least 10 percent of the major schools are breaking the rules. Coaches and athletic directors, aided by alumni, search out the choicest players and recruit them with the agility and skill of quarterbacks. To get a star lineman, one southeastern school paid off the mortgage on his parents' home. A highly sought player was told that an alumnus would "buy" the player's complimentary tickets for the next four years, at $2,000 per season. Coaches whose teams win are glorified in the press—even those on probation for violating the rules.

Ethical and moral standards erode under the relentless pressure of our tempting, highly visible affluence. Television and magazines spread the good life before us—"Go now, pay later"—and a credit card is a magic wand, an "Open Sesame" for the cornucopia of goodies displayed in vivid color. The focus is on satisfying our own needs, lavishly.

Reasoning at the level of self-interest alone tends to drive fees and prices up and ethical standards down. Most professional people are charging what the traffic will bear, but the traffic is beginning to jam under the burden of medical, dental, and legal fees that only the well insured or the very rich can afford.

According to a congressional report, in 1974 surgeons performed more than 2 million unnecessary operations, at a cost of almost $4 million. "Costs, Risks and Benefits of Surgery," a study by 34 medical experts released in 1977, argues that the costs and risks to the patient often outweigh the benefits of surgery and pointed to appendectomies, tonsillectomies, gall bladder and hernia surgery, and certain types of breast and heart surgery, as cases in point.

If a doctor tells Beverly Brown that she needs surgery, she'll probably take his word. She shouldn't; according to a five-year study by Dr. Eugene G. McCarty of Cornell University Medical College, chances are one in three that the doctor is wrong. Hysterectomies rank high on the list of frequently performed and often unnecessary operations—at the present rate, more than half of American women over 65 will soon be minus a uterus.

A cushion of insurance coverage insulates most doctors and patients from the real inflationary effects of escalating fees. This pad of insurance money also encourages expedient thinking—to pass the buck, literally, and ignore the ultimate effect of our actions. A cartoon in *Saturday Review* recently made an acid visual comment on this situation: It showed a parade of hospital personnel moving past a row of patients whose beds were giant cash registers, with rows of escalating figures on each headboard.

When decisions are made at an expedient, Stage Two level of ethical reasoning, corporate morality is motivated solely by the hard facts of profit and loss. We program the computers and make boardroom decisions without consideration for such vagaries as possible damage to the environment or the ultinate welfare of our customers. Dewey said that corporations tend to become machines for carrying on business and in consequence are as powerful and as incapable of moral considerations as any other machines.

Often cited as an example of corporate Stage Two reasoning is a retort made by "Engine Charlie" Wilson to a congressional hearing committee when, as president of General Motors, he sought confirmation as Secretary of Defense in 1953. The congressmen asked him whether his concern for the welfare of General Motors might conflict with his responsibility to the country as a whole. Wilson indignantly replied, "What's good for General Motors is good for the country!"

Seen from the perspective of the 1970s, Wilson's statement—while undoubtedly sincere—indicates the kind of Stage Two moral judgment that confuses self or corporate interest with the larger interests of society. (Eighteen years later, President Lyndon Johnson used Wilson's words to congratulate Reverend Leon Sullivan on his appointment as the first black to sit on the Board of Directors of General Motors. "Now," said the president, "what's good for General Motors really *is* good for America!")

Judgement based on corporate self-interest can lead to some curious examples of double-think, of holding opposing concepts or pursuing two opposing interests simultaneously. For example, during World War II, German firms owned by International Telephone and Telegraph (ITT) built and operated plants making bombers for the Nazi war machine, while their American counterparts designed and manufactured a high-frequency directional finder that enabled the United States forces to detect and destroy German U-boats.

At the same time, ITT was improving its relations with the Third Reich by maintaining its telephone cables between Berlin and Argentina; these provided one of the few links that allowed German agents to report the movements of allied convoys. With the information thus transmitted, German submarines and Focke-Wulf bombers could intercept and attack the convoys.

When the war ended, ITT had to apply to the Allied Occupation Forces control in Germany to get formal repossession of its German firms; this was achieved with the cooperation of ITT men in uniform. Further, a public relations campaign was launched deliberately to submerge the history of ITT's association with the Nazis, Focke-Wulf bombers, and the SS. An ironic postscript was added some 20 years later, in 1967, when the company requested compensation from the United States government for damage done to their German plants by American bombers in World War II. The government, reasoning that the bombers had indeed destroyed American property, paid ITT $27,000,000 including $5,000,000 for the Focke-Wulf factories, which had built bombers for the Luftwaffe. The fact that these factories furnished war materials used *against* the United States and its allies and were damaged as a result of that war was ignored.

Self-fixated Stage Two thinking can lead businesses to ignore their responsibility for damage to the environment in general and even for direct harm to their customers. We constantly receive fresh reinforcement of our growing concern that we live in a jungle of toxic substances: dangerous chemicals in our food, our clothing, our cosmetics—products we use daily and have believed to be harmless turn out to conceal all manner of dangerous chemicals. It's getting to be like those densely drawn trees in puzzle pictures for children: How many wild animals are peeking at you from the leaves? New dangers are announced almost weekly. Researchers discover agents that can cause cancer or sterility or lung damage, an alphabet soup of chemicals whose initials resemble each other and make it hard for us to keep them straight.

More than 12,000 compounds are already on the toxic substance list: Fifteen hundred are suspected of causing tumors, while 30 compounds currently in use are known to be carcinogenic—including certain brands of plastic seat covers, high-energy transformers, decaffeinated coffee, and hair dyes. One confused consumer said he'd read so many terrible things about all the products that could cause cancer that he'd have to give up reading.

The plight of the populace at the hands of unscrupulous corporations is by no means exclusive to the American scene. In the 1950s and 1960s, residents of Minamata, Japan, began to develop severe nerve and brain damage in a syndrome known locally as "the strange disease." Even after the cause became known, it took years of strong and continuing public pressure to induce the Chisso Petrochemical Corporation to stop pouring wastes containing dangerous concentrations of mercury into Minamata Bay. The nutrients in the waters, and therefore the sea animals and fish that fed there, were contaminated with the deadly substance. The people of Minamata, who consumed the fish from the bay, were at the natural end of that lethal food chain.

More than twenty years have passed since Minamata first became aware of the mysterious neurological disorders that afflicted thousands of its people and contributed to 192 deaths. Doctors estimate that more than 10,000 people were directly affected by the Minamata pollution; additionally, there are many deformed and retarded children as a result of the mercury poisoning of pregnant women.

Chisso Petrochemical Corporation could be said to have expressed acute Stage Two reasoning in this instance, although no more so than a chemical plant in the Brazilian state of Bahia, which until 1976 had for years been polluting the Bay of All Saints with even larger quantities of mercury than that found in Minamata Bay. The government, discovering that the waters of the bay contained nineteen times the maximum concentration of mercury regarded as safe by the U.S. Environmental Protection Agency, brought an action against the plant. But even after $20,000 in fines and a citation ordering them to desist, the plant was slow to comply. It was necessary to issue still another restraining order and to fine the operation a second time before effluents were brought down to the required limit. Considering that cases of the slow-developing Minamata disease were still appearing in Japan six years after Chisso discontinued discharging high levels of mercury, it may be that residents in the area of the Bay of All Saints have a heavily mortgaged future.

Corporate Stage Two reasoning sets up the ongoing struggle between manufacturers and the authorities charged with regulating them. Unhappily, the resources of those whose job it is to protect public health are inadequate to the need and far inferior to the financial clout of large corporations. Further, public agencies are constrained by Stage Five considerations such as fairness and due process. For example, the U.S. Food and Drug Administration rightly requires prolonged testing and public hearings before it can take action against a manufacturer of toxic or carcinogenic products; meanwhile, those products remain on the market. And damage to the environment can become severe and irreversible before those charged with protecting it can call a halt. Ironically, it is this Stage Two reasoning on the part of corporations that compels tax-costly policing in the first place. In the long run, extreme Stage Two behavior by both businesses and individuals can be self-defeating.

In a thesis prepared for the Graduate School of Business Administration at Harvard University and with research supervised by Kohlberg, Al Erdynast (1973) did some interesting work with a group of distinguished businessmen attending a seminar at the university. According to Erdynast's findings, the traditionally low-morality stereotype of business executives was unwarranted, despite the low level of morality so often exhibited by the corporate mind.

Notwithstanding the prevailing belief that businessmen are interested only in their corporate or personal self-interest—defining right action only as that which serves self-interest, a typical Stage Two mode of thinking—Erdynast found that none of the executives he interviewed scored as low as Stage Two. His study indicated that all but one were capable of at least some form of Stage Four reasoning and that the majority were capable of some degree of Stage Five thinking.

In contrast, a 1977 survey conducted by the *Harvard Business Review* (Brenner and Molander) turned up different evidence. While 80 percent of the executives polled agreed that "business people should try to live up to an absolute moral standard," fully 50 percent, when questioned further, felt that their bosses (not they, of course) were interested only in results and were not particularly concerned whether those results were obtained ethically or otherwise.

When we asked Kohlberg about the discrepancy between Erdynast's findings and the response to the *Harvard Business Review*'s questionnaire, he replied that obviously business people, like everybody else, reason at all levels. However, he mentioned the important factor of "moral atmosphere" in a company: a tendency in some business organizations to promote regression to a lower stage of moral judgement regardless of the stage of morality reached by individual executives. The powerful Stage One pull of obedience to authority or to an existing policy often wins out over higher levels of reasoning.

To understand any game, you must first consider how it's scored. Corporations are for the most part scored by their record of profit and loss—the Stage Two emphasis on self-interest, on performing a service to get a specific return. John Dewey believed that we have to pass laws that would make it worthwhile for corporations to act in the public good as well as in their own. He wrote, "When ethical principles can be translated into legal restraints, law helps the morally disposed to maintain those principles and frees them from unscrupulous competition" (1932, p. 521). In other words, if you install expensive equipment to keep from polluting the atmosphere, a law can keep your competitors from having an unfair advantage, by requiring them to install the same kind of equipment.

When personal or corporate interests are involved we can try to take off the blinkers that keep us focussed only on profit, and consider honestly whether "what's good for General Motors" is also good for the country. We can argue, discuss, debate—see ourselves in the role of customer or just innocent bystander. How would it look from there?

The thinking of the group is not likely to change for the better if the thinking of each individual does not change. The process of individual moral development, of shifting to a higher ground with a wider view of society's interests is a way of approaching marketplace problems that afflict everyone: inferior or dangerous products; changing a spark plug but charging for a tune-up; performing a surgical operation of dubious value; going to court just for the fee; insisting that the right to pollute is a necessary part of doing business.

Instead of asking, "What's in it for me?" the reasoning could be shifted to "What's in it for all of us?"

◤ THE VITA-GOLD DILEMMA—A DISCUSSION OF OPTIONS

To keep the report quiet and modify the product, considering only the welfare of the company, would be Stage Two reasoning. You could rationalize this practical step with the ideas that there is a good chance that Vita-Gold is harmless to humans or that the experiment could have been incorrectly performed.

Worrying about the possibility of physical harm to the customers and balancing that against the jobs of the people depending on you, concerned about their welfare—seeing the problem in terms of the relationships involved, trying to be a responsible employer as well as an ethical businessman, would indicate Stage Three reasoning.

Concern with the legal aspects, with the fact that no law and no rules have been broken, and trying to follow correct procedures, possibly to modify the product as well as having it retested, would show Stage Four reasoning.

At Stage Five, there would be concern with the greatest good of society—there are far more customers than employees, and for their protection you would be inclined to make the report public and take back all the Vita-Gold that is still unsold.

Interlude One

Adults at Low Stages of
Moral Development

 Fran and Jeff Edwards are sitting over breakfast coffee, each with a section of the morning newspaper. He shakes his head.

JEFF: These days you need a tranquilizer to read the paper. Listen to this stuff—child prostitutes, kiddie porno movies—a headline about a 27 percent increase in rape. And here's one about five hostages shot—an old woman beaten to death for a few bucks. It's a real zoo out there.

FRAN: Some of it's not so far out there—it's right here! One of our own ministers has ripped off a few thousand dollars in a food stamp racket—our county planning commissioner and the district attorney have been indicted on conspiracy and bribery charges. Plus the principal at Lincoln High School is charged with hit-and-run driving. . . .

JEFF: (Shakes his head) Everywhere you look—fraud in the Veterans Administration, the school lunch program . . . respectable businessmen hiring torches. . . .

FRAN: What's a torch?

JEFF: A professional arsonist—a fire setter. I heard one interviewed who claims he can make a million dollars a year. It's easy, he says—business is very good.

FRAN: Talk about respectable businessmen—what's more respectable than a Swiss bank? Listen to this one—"Swiss Credit Bank hit by scandal—losses estimated at four hundred million."

:FF: I guess there are just a few of us left, honest people brought up the old-fashioned way.

RAN: Tell me about it! What about those things you fixed up for your income tax, the phony receipts?

:FF: That's different. Only an idiot pays more tax than he needs to. Anyway, it all evens out.

RAN: Not reporting the cash you get on those weekend installation jobs? What makes it different? How does it even out?

:FF: Don't be so preachy. Do you pay Ana Maria's social security? It's not even legal for her to be working for you.

RAN: She needs the job. She's supporting four children in Mexico.

We've seen how Stages One and Two are normal and predictable in childhood and early adolescence. But this same kind of reasoning is found, although less frequently, in adults. Many of them are leading useful lives; others are constantly in difficulty with the law because of their moral perspective. Criminal offenders are remarkably lower in moral judgment development than are nonoffenders. The majority (75 percent) of noncriminal adolescents and young adults are at Stage Three or Four, while the majority of delinquents and criminal offenders are at Stages One or Two.

It's important to remember, however, that the theory of stage development is concerned with ways of *thinking,* not with types of personalities. It's important to avoid using the stages as labels to fasten on ourselves or others. When stage development theory was explained to one school official who had many problem students, he said, "We always knew they were sons of bitches; we just didn't know they were Stage Two sons of bitches."

This approach can also push people into the trap of self-labeling. Reformatory inmates in California are routinely "Ileveled" according to interpersonal maturity levels of ego development as worked out by psychologist Jane Loevinger. When Kohlberg interviewed one of the inmates and asked him about himself, the man replied, "I'm a Level Three manipulator." Kohlberg said: "That's what they've labeled you—is that what you really are?" "Oh, it's not so bad being a manipulator," the man went on. "I just don't like being locked up with the other manipulators."

Categorizing can be misleading and simplistic—too often we confuse the structure of our thinking with the content. We are not "bad" people at any level, simply people with different perspectives on the world and different reasoning about moral problems.

If development of moral reasoning is logical, natural and beneficial, as the stage development theorists claim, why do some individuals fail to reach the higher stages? Apparently, moral growth doesn't occur spontaneously, as does physical growth. It depends on having enough positive, growth-producing experiences in our lives. Adults who are still reasoning at the lower stages haven't had enough of those experiences. They haven't lived in a situation where seeing things from another's point of view is encouraged or in an environment where logical thinking is stimulated and people take responsibility for making the moral decisions that influence their moral world. They haven't been exposed to conflict about moral decisions—not just emotional conflict, but real discussions that make them aware of other viewpoints and challenge their thinking.

Every society has produced people who don't fit into conventional boundaries of right and wrong, who typify the lowest levels of moral judgment. In some societies, these are the people on top: leaders who grasp and hold power with murder, intrigue, bribery, use fear and torture without regard to a moral code. Morality to such people is for the weak, for the followers.

Sometimes it seems that people at war with society, those

who turn to crime or exploitive, egocentric behavior, have been appearing in increasing numbers in the 1960s and 1970s. Where do *they* fit on a scale of moral development? Some of them are even below Stage One, at a zero level where right and wrong are irrelevant. They see themselves as the center of the universe and regard others purely as a means of gratification. Many are alienated, some are violent, others merely irresponsible. Some are at Stage One, oriented to power; others, at Stage Two, see people as victims to be ripped off before they get ripped off themselves.

When the lights went out in New York in the blackout of 1977, setting the stage for the curtain to go up on a gigantic looting spree, people joined in as if at a fiesta. People helped themselves in a carnival of conspicuous consumption, grabbing whatever could be grabbed, whole families tagging along, small children, grandmothers, friends, and neighbors. When the excitement subsided, sociologists, psychologists, futurists, editorial writers, took out their slide rules and charts and retroscopes and went to work. Why did it happen? What was the reasoning behind it? Futurist Herman Kahn, director of the Hudson Institute, said in a *Time* magazine article (1977): "They have no idea of what moral standards are. This 'suppressed rage' idea is crap. This kind of reasoning will make the same thing happen all over again."

Much of it was typical of behavior based on Stage One or Two reasoning—egoistic, childlike, concerned with immediate reward. Many people at Stage One don't really feel part of society. We all have to live by rules we didn't make, rules enforced by parents, bosses, police. And many Stage One and Two adults come from the bottom of the social structure, from the rural and urban poor of all races, victims and protagonists in the war of the streets, the muggings, the quick fixes—those who have daily familiarity with violent crime.

It's difficult, however, to see how principles of justice and morality can be expected to flourish here, with the patterns of crime and deprivation and a scarcity of models for reasoning at a higher stage, given the fact that our larger society is so thoroughly cross-hatched with immoral, unethical behavior at every level. We read the bigger, blacker headlines about violence at gunpoint, the frightening increase in juvenile crime. But there are other headlines about white-collar crime, computer crime, crimes committed by middle-class and upper-class people who live in stable, conventional environments. For every legitimate business, there's a mirror-image rip-off—capitalizing on the energy crisis by selling fraudulent solar heating devices or collecting in advance for a streamlined windmill generator that never arrives.

This terrifying increase in white-collar crime and the widening incidence of unethical and illegal behavior at every level of society should keep us from any holier-than-thou feeling when we look at problems of delinquency and street crime. Our moral behavior depends on so many factors: the pressures of circumstance, psychological stress, and—for all our founding fathers' egalitarian principles—economic considerations determine not only who falls from grace but also who is spared the consequences.

"Look at Bernard Bergman, the nursing-home operator," complained one of the prisoners interviewed in Susan Sheehan's book, *A Prison and a Prisoner* (1978). "He was responsible for more human misery than I've ever caused. His sentence for running all those terrible nursing homes was four months. And look at Nixon. He tried to steal the Bill of Rights and got a pardon. I only wish to God that when I was younger I'd had someone to teach me economics and banking. Then I could have stolen millions of bucks with a few strokes of the pen and maybe been sent away only once for a couple of years."

In *Man for Himself,* psychologist Erick Fromm (1960) talks about the power of destructiveness. Ethics, he says, is concerned primarily with the problem of irrational hate, the passion to destroy or cripple life. The degree of destructiveness corresponds to the degree in which the unfolding of our capacities is blocked; the outcome of unlived life. Humans have the potential to grow and become destructive only if this potential is blocked.

There's a new concept in criminology, related to the stage theory of moral development, that says criminals are criminals because of how they think, not because they are insane, come from broken homes, are poor, watch too much television, or are involved in drug abuse. According to this theory, criminals have patterns of reasoning that begin as early as age three; they lie in order to gain power or secrecy; they think they are better than others and own the world.

This is the theory of Dr. Stanton Samenow, co-author of a study of "The Criminal Personality" who sees morality as a product of a special kind of thinking. In a 1977 Los Angeles Times interview he said criminals have no concept of injury to others; they may be aware of conscience, but this awareness operates only intermittently. At least one in five such people, according to Samenow, can be taught new patterns of thinking to handle this "criminality," just as alcoholics can learn to manage alcoholism.

The criminal is usually "an intelligent, energetic person who has been irresponsible and unaccountable since childhood," says Samenow. He believes criminals *need* to learn responsibility, can be most effectively treated by helping them to give up their old ways and start to build self-respect. This idea is similar to the stage development concept of stimulating individuals who are fixed at early stages by challenging their ideas, helping them examine their thinking and conduct, in effect changing their patterns of reasoning through exposing them to better ones.

High levels of moral development and obedience to law don't always go hand in hand. The Nazis who followed orders were "law-abiding," as were the Scribes and Pharisees. There is often a conflict between the law and justice, and at each new stage of moral judgment the difference becomes more apparent.

Stage Three

Conformity
"Nice ladies and good old boys"

◪ **Carole's Dilemma** Suppose you were Carole Wheatley, an officer with Pacific Finance Company. You and your husband Lou have been married for fourteen years, and you have three children. At the office, you are offered a promotion to district manager, with a substantial increase in salary and prestige as well as greater responsibility. The new job would involve a certain amount of travel. You love your work and believe that you would like the new position even more.

But Lou isn't happy with the idea. He points out to you that David, five, still sucks his thumb on occasion and that Katie, thirteen, is going through a particularly difficult stage. He feels that it will make all the children very insecure to have their mother away so much of the time, and he's sure that the quality of family life will suffer. However, you have an excellent housekeeper who is reliable and affectionate with the children, and you are sure that the amount of traveling you'll have to do won't make that much difference to the family. As a working wife and mother, you claim that if the situation were reversed Lou wouldn't hesitate to accept the promotion.

What should you do? Why?

(See page 52 for a discussion of options.)

At Stage Three, people are concerned with their own groups; they want the group's approval. Morality means doing what is sanctioned by society, following the rules and the conventions, maintaining loyalty and trust, being concerned with people and their feelings. Stage Three people try to live up to group standards and stereotypical ideals of behavior; they strive to follow appropriate role models and to abide by the accepted rules for suitable conduct. And what are those rules? We all know what they are: You must try to be a good person, a nice boy, a good chairperson, a good husband. A good mother—in the view of all the other mothers on the block—cooks delicious meals, bakes brownies, does the mending, and never gets upset or out of sorts, even if she has a job outside the home. A good mother will even listen to her child's interminable description of the movie he or she saw on television last night, and with loving attention too.

Our friend Mark, now age 15, whose comments at Stages One and Two were reported in previous chapters, is asked once again how he feels about the Captain, the Troublemaker, and the near-suicidal mission. Mark's Stage Three reasoning: "The captain wants to be a good officer and he cares about his men, so he should pick the one he thinks would do the best job. Any good soldier, if his heart was in the right place, would want to help his buddies and would do what was best for all of them."

Just so. And that's why Stage Three is identified traditionally as the "good boy, nice girl" level of reasoning. Solidarity with the group is paramount. There are "good old boys," affable, pleasantly conforming regional types, who act out long-held patterns of behavior; and there's the "old-boy" network, the select ingroup of men from the same class, the same school, the same background, who sponsor, help and promote each other's careers.

The same behavior occurs among women too. When Peggy, just 19, arrived in New York City and got her first job, she unwittingly became part of a peer group of office girls who looked out for each other's interests. Although the Brooklyn and Bronx accents of the other women sounded to Peggy almost forbiddingly tough at first, she soon felt as comfortable with them as she had with her friends back home.

When the boss singled Peggy out to remain after hours every night for some special work, the group became aroused. They knew Mr. Hurley from experience, worried about Peggy's youth and small-town lack of sophistication, and decided to intervene. Appointing themselves her protectors, for many nights they took turns waiting, one each evening, until Mr. Hurley would let Peggy off. "You can go home now," Hurley would call out to the volunteer duenna who sat quietly at the rear of the office.

"Oh, that's OK," each would reply in her turn. "I'm waiting for Peggy. We're having dinner together."

"It might be a while."

"That's all right," the duenna would reply. "I'll wait."

They were working girls together in an exploiting world, and they accepted Peggy as one of them, their friend. Her own mother could not have been more concerned for her welfare.

After a couple of weeks of this Hurley gave up, and Peggy once again left the office with the others at five.

Of course, solidarity has many faces, and another of Peggy's adventures in the big city drew her attention to a different sort of Stage Three conformity. It was her first shopping visit to Gimbel's Department Store. The sale going on there was like nothing she'd ever seen in Henson's Drygoods in Sioux Falls, South Dakota. There were no dressing rooms, and everyone was wrestling for the merchandise; Peggy saw two women almost rip a dress to pieces when they grabbed it simultaneously. Elbows flew—it was real combat. When Peggy inadvertently bumped into a large, heavy women, she apologized, just as she had always done back home. The woman looked at her with exasperation. "If you have to be so goddam polite," she said, "why don't you shop in Lord and

Taylors?" Peggy was not performing properly in the role of a dedicated bargain tracker.

At Stage Three, there's a need to be seen as "good" by others, to be "good" in your own eyes. Unconventional behavior is frowned on—what if everybody did that? In living up to the group's idea of your role, you follow the rules even if it works against your own self-interest. There's a focus on mutual trust, strong personal relationships, shared values. If we do something that would normally be judged as undesirable for the sake of a personal relationship, it can be excused. Helen was a fragile, somewhat timid girl when she married Earl, but Earl soon changed all that. He loved to hunt and fish on wilderness treks, he loved to get under a car or truck and fix it up, no matter how much oil dripped on him, and he loved to have Helen with him, whatever he was doing. Many of Helen's friends disapproved of her unladylike behavior, and her mother, too, was a little shocked at Earl's rough ways and Helen's going along with him. But the older woman understood Helen's determination to be close to her husband, and she certainly approved of that.

Intentions are important. If we mean well, the consequences of our actions won't be quite so harshly judged. Yet it's hard to challenge injustice if it's approved of by everyone around us or by those in authority.

You remember our college friend Derek and his noisy party. At this stage, Derek would probably continue the racket if he felt that most of the people in the building were in his age group and wouldn't really mind. But if someone from that age group pointed out that it was a bit late and noisy, even for his own generation, Derek would bring the festivities to a conclusion.

At Stage One, we do something for someone because we expect a reward, or because we were ordered to do it, or because we might be punished if we don't. At Stage Two, we would do the same favor because we might need a favor in return from that person some day. At Stage Three, we do the favor because we want to make the person happy. It's someone we love, a relative or a friend, a part of our group, and we care. We don't expect anything in return—except, perhaps, approval.

At this stage, the group supports us, helps us to behave more responsibly, and provides us with a warm feeling of belonging, of being fitted into our proper place. Seen from outside, all this warmth and solidarity can look very much like prejudice and intolerance. Inside, however, it may be nothing more than a limited perspective. Lillian Smith, in *Killers of the Dream* (1949), describes the kind-hearted ladies of her mother's sewing circle and their endless tasks—crocheting for the foreign missions, full of good works, but ignoring the racism and discrimination in their own town. Stage Three is the level of conformity, where we view other groups or societies as outsiders, as unbelievers, possibly even as enemies. Some of us at this stage even take on negative morals in order to blend more fully into the group—a gentleman, after all, doesn't like to make a display of virtue. Many people prefer to be thought of as good fellows rather than as virtuous snobs and choose to laugh at cruel ethnic jokes rather than be thought stuffy or square.

A friend likes to tell a story about a civil rights fund raising party in Los Angeles in the 1940s, at which her family singing group had been asked to entertain. They had recently arrived in Los Angeles to try for a career as a professional jazz quintet, and they were glad of the exposure. As she and one of her sisters sat together between numbers on a bench near the orchestra, they were approached by a very short, middle-aged black man. In their Midwestern home town, there weren't many blacks, and there was a provincial attitude about racial mixing. Neither she nor her sisters had ever been to a dance with black people before, and they were self-conscious but anxious to do the proper thing.

When the short man asked her to dance, she smiled and stood. As she describes it, "In those days, you danced *with* someone, arms politely enfolding each other. And even though

I'm average-size I could easily gaze over his head as he steered me around the floor. After he returned me to the bench, he stopped to chat with a friend and then moved back toward us, looking purposefully at my sister Jane, who is a good head taller than I am. She whispered in my ear, 'I'm not going to dance with that man. If he comes over here, I'm not going to do it.'

"I muttered back, 'You can't do that. You can't refuse to dance with someone just because he's black.'

"She said, 'Black? Black? Who cares about that? He's a foot shorter than I am. I'd feel like a fool.'"

My friend always smiles at herself at that point in the story. "There I was," she says, "so anxious about racism and discrimination and all those things, urging my sister toward her moral duty, and none of that was even on her mind. She was self-conscious about her height and scared to death about appearing ridiculous, which makes sense in most seventeen-year-olds, but she was as color-blind and free of prejudice as a baby. She saw that man as a person—a short person, I grant you—but not as a color or a pattern or an outsider." In short, sister Jane may have had her youthful problems, but closed group thinking wasn't one of them.

Mothers and fathers all over the country say to their children: "Be nice, for heaven's sake, be nice; don't get into fights; don't get into trouble, know your place; marry a nice Jewish girl . . . a nice Catholic girl . . . a nice black boy; don't go outside the group; don't challenge authority; don't make waves." Parents the world over say just the same. It's an impulse that grew from a need to keep the children safe in order to ensure their survival, and it can lead us, as adults, into the kind of crowd behavior that leads to extremes—fascism, Nazism, McCarthyism—"going along" carried to the ultimate dimension.

Peer groups and all personal relationships are important at Stage Three, and delightful and supportive exchanges happen at this level. The problem, however, is that the caring has limitations. The closed circles created at Stage Three can lead to discrimination and prejudice.

Sororities and fraternities provide fun and frolic and improved social skills for some students; they also engender deep hurts for those who are invited and inspected and found wanting: "We're in and you're out, buster." Barbara, freshly initiated into Kappa Omega, found herself sitting in her first meeting in a circle of powerful active members to whom she had meekly deferred during her year as a pledge. Her childhood friend, Petra, had not been initiated with Barbara's pledge class because she hadn't made the required grade-point average. Barbara listened in mounting discomfort as the group began to discuss Petra and the advisability of expelling her because of her poor academic performance. Moreover, the girls didn't think she was really *right* for Kappa Omega. Suddenly Barbara heard herself saying that Petra really was pretty outrageous, that she'd even come drunk to chemistry class one afternoon. A vote was taken, and it was decided to expel Petra from the sorority.

When the excitement was over, Barbara regarded herself with disbelief. How could she have done that? Even though Petra *was* eccentric and unpopular, even though she was all the things the other girls said she was, Barbara was supposed to be her *friend*—one of the few Petra had at college. Barbara was torn between two kinds of Stage Three affiliations—loyalty to the group, and loyalty to a friend.

Barbara despised herself, her lack of guts, her willingness to go along with the cruelty of expelling Petra. In the meeting, she had thought only of being like the other girls, doing what they approved, ensuring that all would be smooth and homogeneous in the group. She'd let slide her awareness that Petra very much needed the sort of acceptance that membership in the sorority was giving her. Ten years later, Barbara and Petra are still friends, but Barbara will admit that her conscience still troubles her whenever she evokes the painful memories of her betrayal of Petra.

Our moral reasoning often develops ahead of our courage. How we would love to be noble and valiant and true, just as we see ourselves in our daydreams. All too often the reality is much less glorious; yet we know we can do better. In Barbara's experience with the sorority, she was learning group loyalty and making new friendships, but the experience stifled her courage to defend her friend. When she was a little older, she realized that she'd had more power than she'd imagined and could have explained Petra's background and difficult home life to the others. She could have persuaded the girls to give Petra another chance—if she had trusted herself more. Instead, she is stuck with an image of herself as a Judas, a betrayer of one who trusted her.

At Stage Three, people may be unable to look at moral dilemmas and resolve them from the perspective of the whole society. Social interaction is limited largely to group relations based on sentiment, and political problems are viewed simplistically.

No matter what our level of moral reasoning, we have a powerful and very human tendency to divide society into Us and Them, into "in" groups and "out" groups. This tendency is most pronounced at Stages Three and Four—Stage Four just takes in more territory. According to John Dewey, at these levels we act for the group primarily because we do not conceive of our own good as being distinct from that of the group. We acquire the morality of our social group along with our other social customs as imperceptibly as we inherit our speech patterns. Our actions are only partly guided by intelligence; they are just as much due to habit or to accident. The group trains us to act in the ways it approves, and it holds us by all the means in its power.

In our own class, sex, or nation, we feel we are in the right, supported by moral principles; each side thinks the other is guided by personal desire or by obstinacy. The weakness of this reasoning is that the pressure of habit and custom loom large while access to freedom is minimal. The power of the group holds us up, but it can also hold us back.

An important flaw in the reasoning pattern at Stage Three

is an inability to handle conflicts in society's role expectations. A doctor has a terminally ill patient who is in great pain and begs for an end to her suffering. An ideal doctor is expected to help people, to relieve their pain and suffering; in this role, the doctor should grant the woman's request. But a doctor is also expected to prolong life and has taken an oath to do so. Which of these roles should the doctor fulfill?

There is a tremendous pressure to play well the roles to which we are assigned. Consider an experiment done by Philip Zimbardo (1972) at Stanford University in 1971. Zimbardo was interested in learning what it means psychologically to be a prison guard or a prisoner. He screened over 70 student volunteers to find 24 young men who were mature, emotionally stable, normal, intelligent college students from middle-class homes. None had a criminal record; none had ever been in prison.

By a flip of a coin, the students were divided into two groups at random, half as "guards" and half as "prisoners," in a space designated as a "prison yard." The experiment was designed to last for several days, and in the first day the "guards" were exhibiting brutal and callous behavior that had not been suggested by the experimenters; they treated their charges as less than human. Meanwhile, the "prisoners" readily became meek and traumatized by the climate of prison life. Although they were free to leave the experiment at any time, they seemed almost hypnotized, held in place by the power of the subservient roles assigned to them and the assertive behavior of the "guards."

Zimbardo had to release three prisoners in the first four days because they were crying hysterically, confused in their thinking, and severely depressed. At the end of six days, he called the experiment off because of the frightening results. Zimbardo now says that he canceled the experiment not only because of the horror of the "prison yard" but also because of a realization of his own. "I could easily have traded places with the most brutal guard," he says, "or become the weakest prisoner, full of hatred at being so powerless that I couldn't eat, sleep, or go to the toilet without permission of the authorities" (p. 6). Of prisons, Zimbardo says that the mere act of assigning labels to people and putting them into a situation where those labels acquire validity is sufficient to bring forth pathological behavior.

We are all capable of persecuting others who do not conform to what we see as the social norm—strangers, heretics, traitors—as long as such persecution is sanctioned by our group or by society as a whole. Our own group, our own country, is in the right for whatever reason: It is the majority, or is in tune with the power structure, or espouses doctrines that we believe are divinely inspired.

Inner conformity is made visible by outward codes of dress and behavior. The idea that such codes can express whole sets of beliefs dates back to the Spartans of ancient Greece and the Code of Lycurgus. In the present day, the Nazis initially wore brown shirts; Russia's Young Pioneers sported red neckerchiefs. Even the head of state is not immune from these sorts of pressures. In 1977, two Japanese groups—the League to Dress the Emperor and the Foundation for the Promotion of Japanese Dress—publicly called on Emperor Hirohito to shed Western business suits for the traditional broad-sashed, wide-sleeved kimono. The groups complained that the emperor was never seen in kimono on formal occasions but wore instead the trappings of an alien culture. Rokusuke Ei, spokesman for one of the groups, said that the purpose of the movement was to make the emperor a model of Japanese behavior and dress.

The clash of generations in the 1960s and 1970s often turned on the issue of long hair on young men. Long hair was seen not only as a challenge to established custom, but also—more threateningly perhaps—was widely regarded as a deliberate deviation from traditional patterns of masculinity—

which, of course, it was. This was recognized as an assault on long-cherished ideas and ways of thinking—and the assault was double-barreled, since the young men who enraged their elders by wearing their hair in curls to their shoulders were also, as often as not, the anti-war protestors who cried, "Hell, no; we won't go."

Fairly stated, there are many positive aspects in Stage Three that sometimes offset the negations of strict conformity. The group can exude a powerful force on individual advances in reasoning. The force may be authoritarian and puritanical, even judgmental and unforgiving; however, if there are strong feelings of group warmth and love, stimulated by the satisfactions of belonging, a group can move people from the self-serving reasoning of Stage One or Two to the higher level of Stage Three. The pressure not to let your side down, to live up to what is expected, provides a motive that can change behavior and alter moral perception.

Synanon, an organization that in its earlier years had a remarkable record of success in treating drug addicts, alcoholics and other variously disordered people, used group pressure as a technique, a deliberate tool. By means of it, people were pushed from deviant, egocentric behavior into conforming membership in an expanded family, where Stage Three reasoning was the rule.

Members were required to subscribe to a firmly-enforced code of behavior: No drugs, no alcohol, no smoking, no violence. There were even codes to control dress and hair styles. When new members joined the group, their habitual ways of thinking were verbally and ruthlessly attacked in a free-for-all known as "The Game," in which neophytes had to defend old patterns, old ideas, and old concepts and contrast them with prevailing behavior among Synanon veterans. The challenge was laid down "to see how well the older members are doing, how happy we are, how free from destructive habits." The move to this Stage Three level, at which moral values were determined by group codes and reenforced by group approval, brought significant changes for the better in the behavior and attitudes of a great many people.

For a time, it seemed that the level of moral judgment was significantly lifted for many Synanon members as well. And it was—precisely to Stage Three. So that when the group became embattled over legal issues and certain "enemies" of the organization were identified, the group locked together to fight these outside forces that threatened to harm the group. As one former member said when interviewed by the Los Angeles *Times* (1978), "It was like a drumbeat, constant, pervasive, filling the mind constantly. Enemy. Enemy. You can't help but begin to believe it." (p. 23)

Reportedly, according to former members, the mood and attitude of the group was that anyone who would not support Synanon was an enemy, as was anyone who tried to investigate or question Synanon in any way. Members felt threatened. Says one former member: "There were times when the whole community would go on red alert, everyone would stay up all night, there were teams of guards patrolling. Most of it did not prove to be real."

According to the *Times*, commands circulated within Synanon to "get" certain designated enemies. Finally one of these, an attorney who had won a legal judgment against the group, reached into his mailbox one morning and was bitten by a rattlesnake that had been placed there in an apparent murder attempt. Two Synanon members have been arrested and founder Charles Dederick has been charged with plotting to commit murder, but the organization denies any complicity.

Whatever the outcome of these proceedings, we see here that the urge to achieve the group's approval and to conform to its ways is a powerful one. The longing to belong to a superior group exists in varying degrees in us all, as does the impulse to defend and reinforce the integrity of that group—if necessary, by any means at hand. Thus the group power that helped so many people was turned to destructive ends.

While the level of moral reasoning can be raised by the

pressures of group opinion and behavior, this task can also be accomplished in the classroom. Initially, Kohlberg didn't believe that teachers could do much to alter or hasten the process of moral growth except in a passive way, by providing optimum conditions for moral learning. However, Moshe Blatt, a doctoral student at the University of Chicago when Kohlberg was teaching there, became convinced that teachers could encourage and stimulate moral development in the classroom by means of discussions of moral dilemmas, using the Socratic method.

Blatt did a pilot study in 1968 with a Sunday School class of children aged 11 and 12 and followed it up by working with a group selected from four public school classes. These were carefully chosen to include a variety of ages and socioeconomic levels—sixth grade and tenth grade, lower middle class and lower class, both white and black. The discussion groups used Kohlberg's concepts and methods—in all classes the students were reasoning at different stages, and the arguments they used were obviously at differing levels.

In the course of the discussions, the teacher would first support and clarify the arguments that were at a stage *above* the lowest stage among the children. He would take a Stage Three stance if the lowest level were Stage Two. When his Stage Three arguments were apparently understood by the students, the teacher would then challenge them, using new situations and employing arguments at the next higher stage.

Following are excerpts from a transcript of Blatt in action (1968, pp. 9-14). They illustrate his techniques as he encouraged students to define moral issues. In these segments, the class (of disadvantaged 15-year-olds) is arguing about the case of Mr. Jones, whose child, Mike, has been wounded accidentally in the chest. The situation is serious: Mike is bleeding heavily, and his shoes and pants are soaked with blood. Mike's mother, believing her son is dying, begins to scream hysterically. Without hesitation, Mr. Jones lifts his son and runs into the street to try to get a cab, believing that will be quicker than calling an ambulance. But there are no cabs on the street, and Mike's bleeding seems worse. Mike's father sees a man parking his car. He runs over, child in arms, and asks the man to take him and his boy to a hospital. The man replies, "Look, I have an appointment about a job. I'd like to help but I can't." "Give me the keys then," pleads Mr. Jones. But the man refuses. "I don't know you," he says. "I don't trust you." Mr. Jones passes his bleeding child to his hysterical wife, beats up the man, takes his keys and drives off. The man calls the police, who arrest Mr. Jones at the hospital for car theft and aggravated assault.

BLATT: Would you have done that?

STUDENT A: He should have called the ambulance. He can't make nobody do something he don't want to do.

BLATT: The man who refused to give Mr. Jones the car—was he perfectly OK in what he did?

STUDENT B: He could do anything he wanted to do with his own car. [Other students show agreement.] And still, he could just go along. Or he could have helped the man if he wanted to, but only if he wanted to.

BLATT: All right. Mr. Jones stole the car. Does Mr. Jones have the legal right to beat up the man and take his car?

STUDENT B: He doesn't have the legal right, no.

BLATT: No. Because this guy has a right to property, and Mr. Jones obviously has no right to hurt this guy. Now, what was involved on this side? What was Mr. Jones' problem? (Chorus of "The boy.") And there was a case of life, right? (Chorus of "Right.") This guy's right to property conflicts with [Mike's] right to life.

STUDENT C: Yes, but the law doesn't say you can't steal unless somebody's life is involved. The law says you can't steal.

BLATT: So what you're saying is according to the law it doesn't make any difference when you steal. Stealing is stealing, and wrong. OK? (Chorus of "Right.")

STUDENT A: He was wrong to take the car.

STUDENT C: You got to have a reason for what you steal.

STUDENT A: What is a good reason for you doesn't have to be a good reason for somebody else.

STUDENT B: If you were bleeding and your father was running around with you trying to get somebody to take you to the hospital, you know good and well that you want your father to hit that dude and take that car, wouldn't you?

STUDENT A: No!

STUDENT B: Yes, you would. You'd be laying there, bleeding to death, wouldn't you? You'd let your own self die?

STUDENT A: But I'm saying that it's against the law. You took something that wasn't yours.

BLATT: All right, let me ask you, what is the purpose of the law? (Two or three [students] answer, "To protect.") To protect people and their property. In this case, suppose you have here a person whose life is in danger. You say the function of the law is to protect the people. All right. Now, it has to protect life—

STUDENT A: That other man's life may depend on that car too. He has to get a job. If he don't get it, he might die. You have to see what a person thinks is more valuable, a life or a car.

BLATT: So what you're saying is circumstances don't make a difference. Stealing is stealing, no matter what. (Chorus of "No." Another chorus of "Yes.") Defend yourself.

STUDENT A: I will not change my mind. Why should it make a difference? Tell me one good solid reason why it should. That's just like telling a doctor that he should take a man's life so he can save his best friend's life. Like his best friend needs a heart so he's going to go out and kill somebody.

STUDENT D: It's wrong. I'd rather my friend died. Taking somebody else's heart to save his friend's life—

BLATT: But there you're depriving someone of life. You're saying that property equals life?

STUDENT A: He had a good reason but that doesn't mean it's right.

BLATT: What kind of reason are you talking about?

STUDENT E: A moral reason.

STUDENT B: Legally it's wrong, morally it's right. (Argument.)

STUDENT A: We're not arguing moral, we're arguing legal.

BLATT: I want you to consider both, moral and legal. All right. Mr. Jones is brought before the judge. What punishment should Mr. Jones get and why?

STUDENT I: A fine, about a hundred dollars.

BLATT: All right, what's the purpose of punishment? What's the function of punishment?

STUDENT A: So you won't do it again.

BLATT: All right, this is one. Any other reason?

STUDENT A: Satisfy the man.

In this class of 15-year-old disadvantaged students, the discussion focused on Student A's position that taking the car was unjustified, a mixture of Stage One (it's stealing, you get put in jail) and Stage Two (you can't make someone do something he doesn't want to do). Blatt and the other students tried to convince him there can be good reasons, independent of the law, which can be formulated at a Stage Two or Three level, and that you should think of "moral right" and of "good reasons" as well as of legal right.

After a semester of this challenging form of debate, all the students were retested. They showed significant upward change compared to control groups, and they maintained that change when they were tested again a year later. In the various classrooms, from one-fourth to one-half of the students moved up a stage, while there was essentially no change in the control group during the course of the experiment.

An interesting feature of the experiment, Blatt found, was that it was necessary to expose the students not only to the next higher stage of reasoning but also to situations that posed problems and contradictions for the students' *current* moral structure. This tended to make them dissatisfied with the level where they were, stimulating the desire to move upward. Another essential ingredient was an atmosphere of interchange and dialogue in which conflicting moral views were compared in an open, uncondemning way.

Another kind of classroom experiment with Stage Three reasoning was reported in the July 1976 issued of *Psychology Today*.* A high school history teacher named Ron Jones was covering material on Nazi Germany, and his students asked him inevitable questions about the period: "How could so many nightmarish things have occurred under the Nazi regime?" "How could neighbors and friends claim not to have noticed anything when whole Jewish families disappeared?" Jones decided to involve the entire class in seeking out the answers.

Jones taught his students the discipline of learning a new posture while seated at their desks. He began to demand unquestioning obedience and introduced new rules that required students to stand by their desks when asking or answering questions, and always beginning by saying, "Mr. Jones." Soon everyone was popping up with questions and answers, even formerly hesitant pupils. After deliberately creating an authoritarian environment, Jones was shocked to realize how well it worked. His students were responding accurately, were asking better questions, and were more cooperative.

He wrote on the blackboard "STRENGTH THROUGH DISCIPLINE" and "STRENGTH THROUGH COMMUNITY." Jones had his students chant the slogans over and over. He created a salute for class members, the right hand raised to the shoulder, fingers curled. It was called the "Third Wave" salute because the curled fingers looked vaguely like a wave about to break and because beach lore says that each third wave is a large one.

Thirteen curious students from other classes cut them in order to join the original Third Wavers. Membership cards were issued to all 43 students. Three students were assigned

---

*Quoted material reprinted from *Psychology Today* magazine. Copyright © 1976 Ziff-Davis Publishing Company.

to report any members not complying with class rules. This measure proved unnecessary: Twenty students came to Jones voluntarily with tales of other students who hadn't saluted or who had criticized the experiment. The program mushroomed; by noon on the fifth day the auditorium was jammed with more than 200 students. Guards were posted to keep out everybody else. Jones walked to the front of the auditorium and asked the audience "to demonstrate the extent of our training." He saluted, and 200 arms rose in reply. He shouted, "STRENGTH THROUGH DISCIPLINE," again and again, and each time the response got louder and louder. Then Jones started to speak.

"Listen closely," he said. "You've been used, manipulated, shoved by your own desires to where you are now. You're no better or worse than the Nazis we've been studying. You thought you were the elect—better than those outside this room. You bargained your freedom for the comfort of discipline. Oh, you think you were just going along for the fun, that you could extricate yourself at any moment, but where were you heading? How far would you have gone? Let me show you your future."

Jones switched on a rear-screen projector. Pictures of a Nazi rally came on, followed by pictures of people being shoved into vans, pictures of death camps and of people pleading ignorance at the war crimes trials at Nuremberg. Suddenly the film froze on a single frame, with the words: "Everyone must accept the blame. No one can claim that they didn't in some way take part."

Jones resumed his remarks. "In the next few minutes," he said, "perhaps years, you'll have a chance to answer this question. If our enactment of the fascist mentality is complete, not one of you will ever admit to being at this Third Wave rally. You won't admit to being manipulated, to accepting this madness as a way of life. It's a secret I shall share with you."

Human society is always starting afresh, always in the process of renewal. In a changing world, old habits need modifications, no matter how well they have served. As our moral judgment lifts, we rely less on habitual responses to group demands and learn to trust our personal choices; we widen our definition of the word neighbor, encourage individual development where we can and concern ourselves with the happiness and the value of every person.

The positive aspects of Stage Three—loyalty, friendship, good feelings in the group—carry a rich potential for growth beyond their present limits. The group responsibility for its members—the Chinese way of making quicker students in a class responsible for the slow learners, or a community sense of joint responsibility for all the children in it—could be extended outward to take us to a much higher perspective. The group *could* be seen as large enough to embrace the world.

◢ **CAROLE'S DILEMMA—A DISCUSSION OF OPTIONS** If you decide to forego the promotion because you are concerned about your family's welfare and your relationship with them, that would be indicative of Stage Three reasoning.

Should you decide to refuse the promotion because you believe a good mother would want to be at home with her children as much as possible, that would also be typical of Stage Three thinking.

If you opt to accept the promotion because it would be better for you both financially and professionally, that would be closer to a Stage Two point of view.

Or you might decide to accept the promotion in the belief that in the long run the larger salary and your increased satisfaction with your job would make you a better wife and mother, weighing the amount of time you would be away and deciding you could make your children feel loved and secure, could handle both your family and job responsibilities. This would be a Stage Five approach.

Stage Four

Law and Order
"The tyranny of the majority."

◢ **The Angel Dust Dilemma** What would you do if you
were Beverly, a widow living with your 16-year-old son
David in a pleasant suburban home? You and David are good
companions and good friends, as well as mother and son.
You've had some problems, particularly over David's occasional
use of marijuana, but nothing really serious. After all, as David
says, "everybody at school has tried it at least once."

While cleaning David's room one morning, you notice what
looks like marijuana on a shelf behind his nightstand. But this is
different from any you've seen before: It's bright green, without
seeds, and it smells like mint. In the back of the drawer, you find
ten more baggies filled with this stuff. You remember a recent
article about a street drug called Angel Dust—PCP. Sometimes
it comes in liquid form and parsley or mint leaves are soaked in
it. It's a very dangerous substance—prolonged use can cause
permanent brain damage; an overdose could mean death from
respiratory failure. And many of its users have suffered frightening derangements.

When David comes home from school that afternoon, you
confront him with your find. Yes, he admits, it's Angel Dust, but
he says you shouldn't believe all that propaganda about brain
damage. He says he has some because a few of his friends like

to get high on it, and he happens to know a guy who's the best source in town. You insist that David destroy this stuff immediately. David says that if you're going to make such a big deal out of it he'll do as you say. You make him promise not only to destroy what he has but also to have nothing more to do with it. You warn him that if he breaks his promise you'll take some serious action.

A few weeks later, you get a call from an angry neighbor. "My son Bill got a drug from David," the woman says. "We had to put our boy in the hospital—he was in intensive care for three days." You can't believe that David would have done such a thing, but you promise to investigate. "You'd better," the woman says. "Either you put a stop to what your son is doing or I'll call the police myself and turn him in."

When you confront David with the call, he says he's terribly sorry that Bill is in the hospital; he confesses that he did sell him some Dust. You are shocked that your son has broken his promise and is involved with something so lethal. David tries to rationalize, saying he hadn't encountered any problems with the drug before; he says that you and he never have much money for extras, and that he wanted to help. But he swears to you that this time he really will get rid of the stuff and have nothing more to do with dealing.

You are filled with doubt and fear, and feel you must take some kind of action—but what? David has already broken his promise to you once; maybe this time he's learned the seriousness of what he's been doing. But what if he hasn't? Can you turn your own son over to the police? Should you punish him in your own way and count on holding him to his promise? (See page 67 for a discussion of options.)

At Stage Four, we rank our values in terms of how important we see them to be to the functioning of society. Our relationships become part of the larger perspective—the whole social structure. We have a new idea of the system: It's a network of complementary individual roles in which our obligations are defined by the rules. We are concerned with the support and maintenance of authority—an authority dependent on moral conformity by both the leaders and the led.

A more mature Mark, now at Stage Four, has a fresh analysis of the dilemma of the Captain, who needs to send a man on a near-suicide mission: "When you join the service," Mark says, "you know what your place is, you know what your job is, and you know you've got to risk your life. It's the captain's job to make the decisions that are best for his company. And in this case, if he decided that the Troublemaker is the best one to go, then the Troublemaker should not refuse him. The only one that decides right and wrong is society. Society is the one that decides if this captain had the right to make a choice, and either choice he made, society and the law are behind him."

Thus with Stage Four reasoning, "right" is defined by the rules that are binding on us all. Again, there's a concern about those who deviate—what if we all did that? It would throw the whole system out of whack and undermine the basis for our shared expectations, the kinds of behavior we know we can count on from each other. Mutual trust, honesty, and dependability are important. If we can't trust and depend on each other, the whole fabric of society is weakened.

At this stage, our rowdy friend Derek, still passing out the six-packs at that noisy party of his, would end it according to existing rules of the apartment house or of the city code. As long as Derek clearly understood exactly what the rule was, he would abide by it and, at the designated time, send his friends home or quiet them down.

Our understanding and perspective have moved higher, higher than that of the individual or the group or our personal relationships, to focus on what's best for society as a whole. Because the protection of basic values such as life and property requires a general system of order, at Stage Four we rank law and order as superior to any other values that might conflict. And the smooth functioning of society is seen to depend on each of us in the performance of our designated tasks and on our loyalty to the whole.

The story that follows is based on a 1975 newspaper article and is factually presented here, although the names have been changed and the circumstances altered slightly. The attitudes and remarks are from real life, and have about them a strong flavor of Stage Four reasoning.

Bill Murray is standing at the door of the Elks Hall, shaking hands with people from his neighborhood who have turned out for a meeting of Concerned Citizens. More than 300 men and women, mostly middle-aged, take seats facing a banner that spells out "Law—Order—Morality" and wait quietly for the program to begin.

Many of these people are new to this sort of activism. In the question-and-answer segment that begins the evening, one young man says that he's boggled by bureaucracy. Others say that they don't know when or where their city council meets. But they feel that their city is deteriorating, and they want to do something about it.

The main focus is on crime: There are too many tricky ways for criminals to evade the law. The people at the meeting are also concerned about pornography and want it stopped. Crime—particularly strong-arm robberies and youth gang violence—is up 9 percent this year. And, although the number of X-rated movies hasn't increased, the people are worried about the effect they're having. "Pornographic movies, right here on State Street," says Mrs. Reba Thompson. "They let the children in. How? Six dollars, honey. That's all you need."

Murray rises to explain how Concerned Citizens got started. Mrs. Barbara Morgan, a member of Murray's church, founded the group a few months ago. She was worried about burglaries in her neighborhood and threats to her children at school. Mrs. Morgan speaks. "What I did," she says, "was draw up a petition and walk my block. I got 42 signatures, 100 percent."

Murray, sharing Mrs. Morgan's worries, got up a petition of his own, and 159 out of the 162 neighbors he approached signed it. Murray and Mrs. Morgan decided to try for 50,000 signatures on a petition to the city council. It calls for "a highly substantial increase of law enforcement" directed toward robberies, X-rated movies, curfew violations, and gang violence in the streets and on school campuses.

"Basically, it goes back to the home," Mrs. Morgan says. "It started when our mothers started working. We've had 20 years of moral decay of children. There's too much leniency in the schools. School authorities have their hands tied. We need stronger laws, corporal punishment. It's the kids controlling the teachers now."

Police Chief Carl Squires says he understands the group's concern. He's increased the number of patrol cars and added two motorcycle patrolmen. But it's hard to say what the average citizen can do to fight crime. Groups like Neighborhood Watch last for a while and then seem to fizzle out. "Either that or they want to turn into a vigilante committee, and we can't have that."

Emotion runs high. At one point, when Councilman Jay Borden cautions that "crime is a problem that has to be handled with logic and reason," he is nearly shouted down.

Councilman Graham Elkins is introduced as the keynote speaker. "Some communities are clean enough to raise decent families," he says, "and some are Sodom and Gomorrah. The Great White Way is now a human sewer, and, as for Hollywood and Vine, it's a human zoo.

"We need tough laws, tough law enforcement. We need to be as powerful and determined as the forces of crime and evil. We need to repeal the rulings that tie the hands of the police, give out some really stiff sentences. That's the only thing people understand."

The audience gives him a standing ovation.

At Stage Four, doing our duty is important. It is our own individual contribution to upholding the structure of society. This is the level where vast numbers of us are, oriented to law and order and custom: We do things this way because they have always been done this way. This is how our society functions. We try to act in the right way, but we aren't always able to think through all the implications of the values held sacred in our own system. We tend to defend such values emotionally rather than logically because our standards of ethics and morality are not the product of our own thinking and analysis. They derive from the regulation of the state. Morality at this stage is involved with maintaining existing laws and customs. When most of us talk about "law and order," we really mean protecting the status quo. A question about social justice, posed in Kohlberg's research, drew this typical Stage Four response: "If we have law and order, why do we need justice?" Stage Four thinking doesn't provide a rationale for social change or for the creation of new laws.

Just as at every level, many good people reason at Stage Four. As Kohlberg says, there is no validity in judging or grading people as morally better or worse than others—judging people as morally good or bad is not justified within universal moral principles, nor by the concepts of stage development. Stage Four people are concerned with their society, with doing their duty, obeying the rules, paying their bills on time, paying their taxes, helping their neighbors, serving on juries, supporting civic organizations. As such, they form the backbone of every nation.

Take John Blanford, for example. John grew up on a farm in Iowa. He worked his way through college and law school, raised a fine family, served in two wars, was loyal and generous to family and friends, and lent money frequently to his wife's relatives without even mentioning it to her. He was the soul of honor and decency and common goodness, and his perspective was typical of Stage Four. While this in no way limited his loyal and generous nature, it did confine the range of his reasoning as it related to the conventions and customs of the small town in which he grew up. His perception of the world and of his place in it were strictly ordered by the values of his own class, country, and race. He believed that people are poor because they are lazy, yet he gave generously to charities. He could never be consciously unkind; nevertheless, he saw the world in terms of Us and Them.

A profession in which Us and Them thinking is particularly prevalent is that of law enforcement, and for most of us the policeman is our closest contact with law and order, with the authority of the state. The popular image these days is the TV cop, the polite young men of *Adam 12* or the wearier men of *Dragnet,* the free-wheeling Starsky and Hutch, all using their automobile accelerators as their major weapon against crime.

Do police think about the ethical and moral problems implicit in the performance of their jobs? William Ker Muir, Jr. believes that they do and reports his observations in *Police: Street-Corner Politicians* (1977). He notes that some policemen use all the coercion necessary to do the job as they conceive it; others try persuasion or bargaining rather than force. In his book, Muir enumerates the qualities that make for effective police officers: A blend of compassion and strong character; a determination to resist crime and criminality even at the risk of life; professional competence; and sensitivity to the problems faced by the people with whom they are involved.

Muir believes that the best officers are those who hold an essentially tragic view of life, who recognize the human condition with all its problems and difficulties—the limitations of human nature. These officers believe that character is more important than personal attitudes—that, despite the pressures of the job and the hostility encountered in the daily round, good officers must adhere to their ethical standards. There are policemen who, in using maximum force, might be reasoning at Stage One, totally oriented to power; there are others who work with the reciprocity of Stage Two—"Commit a crime and I'll beat you up." But the best officers, in Muir's view, reason at Stage Four or even at Five, upholding the law but protecting the rights of the individuals involved.

In the 1960s, police officers with Stage Four or Five consciousness seemed in short supply under the pressure brought by antiestablishment, antiwar students. A conflict arose for many of us between our traditional law-and-order image of policemen as symbols of help and authority and the brutal, repressive behavior police displayed in many parts of the country. To the young, in the emotional, polarized climate of those days, policemen were symbols of oppression—"pigs." There was rage and fear on both sides, with the inevitable consequences. It's one thing to read about "police riots" in the press or see squads move with tear gas against students on TV; many of us, though, had more vivid confrontations with the violence of those times. Some of us were anguished parents, afraid for our activist children but proud of them too. And some of us were there on the streets, "the people our parents warned us about." And some of us, undergraduates at that time but disengaged, were caught up in the violence whether we wished it or not. Like one student at the University of California, who lived in Isla Vista (the student quarter) during the troubles; one day he walked unaware into a melee, and two deputies chased him into his apartment, smashing his belongings at random.

For his parents and their friends, the sight of the smashed turntable, the broken typewriter, heightened the impact of the headlines of the period, brought closer the shootings at Kent State and the violence on campuses all over the country. Those incidents permanently altered the political attitudes of several generations, although neither camp emerged from those stormy days as either triumphant or "right." What was basically a conflict between Stage Four concepts (police adherence to conventional law-and-order attitudes) and Stage Five concern (students' belief in social justice) descended to a low level of violent, emotional, irrational behavior on both sides.

One of the shortcomings of Stage Four reasoning is that it allows no doubt about whether the policies of the state are moral. They are moral *because* they are the policies of the state.

So what does this do to the concept of the law? Each of the three basic levels of moral development takes a different perspective. At Stages One and Two, the preconventional levels, we obey the law because we'll be punished if we don't. At Stages Three and Four (the conventional levels), we are law-maintaining, actively supporting and upholding the law. Stages Five and Six are characterized by the kind of reasoning that makes laws and, if need be, breaks laws, seeking to enact statutes that will benefit all of society and enhance the quality of justice for everyone.

From the perspective of Stage Four moral reasoning, the law is concerned with maintaining traditional procedures, and our attitude toward it is correspondingly ritualized. Many of these rituals are really games, highly stylized processes the roots of which go back hundreds of years in Anglo-Saxon jurisprudence. It is from this tradition that we derive the hard-won rights we cherish, historical protections from the whims and oppression of kings and other persons of privilege, rights nailed down by revered documents from Magna Carta, signed by King John in the 13th century, to the Bill of Rights. However, many of the law's archaic procedures have little or nothing to do with the pursuit of justice and deal rather with ritualistic or random methods for handling conflicting claims.

In earlier times, parties to a dispute would engage champions to settle the matter in physical combat, in the belief that God would intervene on behalf of the righteous and determine the outcome—a custom dating back almost a thousand years to William the Conqueror. An accused usually fought his accuser, although noblemen might sometimes appoint champions to represent both parties in combat. Certainly women and priests were customarily represented by brawnier types. The practice of dueling stemmed from this idea of personal combat as the most convenient and honorable way of settling a legal dispute. The court might order a duel, not only when a crime had been committed but also to settle an argument of any kind. The litigant with the most skilled or most powerful champion was the winner. There were also trials by torture or duress, and many accused people were flung into a lake on the principle that if they were innocent, God would save them from drowning, just as God would give victory to the appropriate champion.

This tradition of champions is still very much alive in the modern American courtroom, where the person with the smartest or most skilled or most expensive lawyer quite often wins, whatever the merits of his case. Recently, posing the question of what is the greatest American sport, *Time* Magazine dismissed football, baseball, golf, or tennis and named the law—the dramatic contests of the courtroom and excitement heightened by high stakes: liberty, and even life.

By emphasizing winning over truth, the adversary system of justice in this country can give the advantage to the rich, the intelligent, and those willing to fight dirty. Our legal system, far from discerning between the innocent and the guilty, all too often distinguishes instead between winners and losers. But there are some indications that a more advanced moral reasoning about law and justice is gaining support.

Dealing with the thorny, large-scale problems of school integration in Los Angeles County, Superior Court Judge Paul Egly recently complained, "I have lost faith in the advocacy system for this type of proceeding, and I am looking for another way the law gives me." He wanted to move the tangled case out of the hostile atmosphere of the courtroom to a quiet place where reasonable people might find a solution.

Why do such proceedings move so slowly, with such unsatisfactory results? Why can't expert witnesses, skilled lawyers, and a respected, experienced judge come up with a just and equitable solution? Egly believes it is because, under the adversary system, lawyers regard their opponents as enemies who cannot be granted merit or logic in their arguments. Everything is reduced to "my client is right, and yours is wrong," and in the process the search for truth and justice is abandoned.

Our adversary system is an example of Stage Four concern for traditional procedures. A different approach, an engagement of both sides in a mutual effort to achieve justice, such as Judge Egly longed for, would be in conflict with the conventional Stage Four way of regarding problems of law and ethics. A nonadversary approach would be more typical of Stage Five reasoning, which seeks to protect the rights of all members of society and sees justice in terms of fairness rather than victory. Many people who reason at Stage Four do not even understand that there is a difference.

Says F. Lee Bailey, who is usually regarded as an impassioned legal advocate rather than as a legal philosopher: "Our deification of the notion of a 'fair trial' has so far submerged the value of an accurate trial that the latter has no real legal significance. That a trial be 'fair' ought to be a minimum standard, not an ultimate objective; someone ought to have the temerity to ask whether the result was correct, not simply whether the rituals were acceptable."

Concerned lawyers are working to improve and enforce legal codes of ethics, and influential figures such as Chief Justice Warren Burger speak out, putting forth suggestions for new ways to upgrade the legal profession and hold it to the highest standards of conduct. Leon Jaworski, writing a survey of legal ethics in *Ethical Basis of Economic Freedom* (1976), says that the rules governing the conduct of lawyers have changed more in the past dozen years than ever before in history. The adoption in all states of the revised Code of Professional Responsibility, approved by the American Bar Association in 1969 after more than five years of study and debate, was a step in the right direction. Jaworski claims that everyone in the legal profession agrees that lawyers must assume the ethical and public responsibilities of membership.

The American Bar Association's Code of Professional Responsibility

1. A lawyer should assist in maintaining the integrity and competence of the legal profession.

2. A lawyer should assist the legal profession in fulfilling its duty to make legal counsel available.

3. A lawyer should assist in preventing the unauthorized practice of law.

4. A lawyer should preserve the confidences and secrets of a client.

5. A lawyer should exercise independent professional judgment on behalf of a client.

6. A lawyer should represent a client competently.

7. A lawyer should represent a client zealously within the bounds of the law.

8. A lawyer should assist in improving the legal system.

9. A lawyer should avoid even the appearance of professional impropriety.

If these canons were fully implemented, with an emphasis on Item 8—lawyers should assist in improving the legal system—and if the focus of the system were the search for justice, rather than the dueling and gamesmanship that currently occupy the courts, then we could come closer to fulfilling the pledge of "Liberty and justice for all" that we so readily repeat on public occasions with our hands pressed to our hearts.

One of the limitations of Stage Four reasoning is the fact that at this level we don't feel any clear obligation to anyone outside our own order or to those who don't recognize the rules of our order. This loyalty to the existing structure, and a companion concern for that structure's laws, can translate into the most violent acts and the most complete disregard for human rights when those whose rights are violated are seen as enemies of the state. All sorts of repressive acts have proliferated under the justification of national security: genocide, terrorism, the work of the NKVD, the Stalinist purges, Gestapo brutality, the covert and illegal activities of the CIA and the FBI.

In wartime, Stage Four attitudes flourish on both sides with equal conviction: "Our cause is just; we are fighting for the right; God is on our side." However strongly we may idealize the notion of universal brotherhood, it's almost impossible to free ourselves from the bonds of national allegiance to become citizens of the world. From childhood onward, loyalty and obedience to our own country and its laws are driven deep into our consciousness.

In a civil war, these conflicts are peculiarly agonizing, as they set even brother against brother because of differing interpretations of what loyalty means. In the American Civil War, young men of North and South spent their lives on the bloody meadows and ridges of Gettysburg, Antietam, and Bull Run. They believed that they were defending their homes and families and the highest ideals of the society to which they belonged. Six hundred thousand died without a chance to live out normal lives, raise families, and grow old in routine pursuits, rocking away in old age on their front porches.

In Dewey's words, there's no Helen of Troy to provide an impetus for modern warfare. The more horrible and depersonalized war becomes, through the advance of science and technology, the more necessary it is for propagandists to find universal, idealized motives with which to justify it. The love for Helen is replaced by a burning love for one's country, for one's fellows; the hatred of the foe now becomes a hatred for all the unrighteousness and injustice and oppression that the foe embodies.

War becomes insanity, but at the level of Stage Four reasoning it is difficult to admit it. We laugh, but not without tears, at Joseph Heller's *Catch 22* (1955), because it exposes the madness of war, mercilessly slashing holes in the banners we like to see waving above our own troops, bearing such glib slogans as "Honor, Sacrifice, and Courage." And, when Heller writes about profiteering and confusion and people dying because of carelessness or misunderstanding, we don't really care to hear about that.

But, in this century, more and more individuals are questioning government policies that violate their personal convictions. Their model as often as not is Thoreau, who practiced civil disobedience to protest the Mexican-American War and went to jail for it. One hundred and twenty-five years later, hundreds of thousands of young Americans fled the country or were jailed because of their refusal to fight in Vietnam. For most of these, it was an act of individual courage to choose prison or exile rather than serve in a war they believed to be unjust and irrational. Many were reasoning at a higher level than Stage Four conformity to the rules of the nation; they saw the nation's enemy as reluctant, suffering participants in a drama they had not chosen. The stubborn resistance of these young people gradually changed the climate of opinion in this country, and the people themselves helped to stop a war.

That so few of us develop a perspective beyond that of Stage Four loyalty has brought incalculable tragedy, death, and suffering to humanity. The numbers are difficult to absorb. The bloodiest single battle in human history was the first battle of the Somme in 1916: Six hundred and ten thousand British and French soldiers were killed, 420,000 Germans, a total of 1,030,000 lives expended for a few hundred yards of muddy soil. There were 52 million deaths in World War II—120 million in all the wars of the Twentieth century so far.

If we are ever to have done with such statistics, we will require first a massive change of attitude from the unquestioning loyalty to tribe and nation that lies behind those figures.

Stage Four will have to be superseded by a higher level of moral understanding, of allegiance not to one country but to all humanity.

▟ **THE ANGEL DUST DILEMMA—A DISCUSSION OF OPTIONS** If you decided to turn David in to the authorities because he should no longer be allowed to get away with this behavior, you would be reasoning at Stage Two. In this mode, you would argue to yourself that, by breaking his promise to you, David has forfeited his claim on your tolerance of his dangerous and illegal activities.

At Stage Three, you might reason that your relationship with David is strong enough that you can use it to hold him to his promise this time. You would punish him yourself in an appropriate way.

Using Stage Four reasoning, you would probably decide that, in spite of your love for David and your reluctance to involve him with the authorities, he has broken the law, has broken his word to you, and has illegally sold a dangerous drug and risked the life of another person. You would report the matter to the police.

At the level of Stage Five, you may feel the important factor is that what David is doing is part of a pattern that creates great social harm and is immoral as well as illegal. You would decide that official punishment and/or supervision for David—the obligation to report to a law enforcement officer—would be more effective than anything you could do about the problem on your own. Since he's bringing harm to other individuals as well as himself, you'd report the matter to the authorities.

Interlude Two

Cheating
and Whistle Blowing

Fran and Jeff Edwards are in their living room enjoying a nightcap. Their neighbors, the Holmeses, have just left after severely trouncing the Edwards at bridge.

FRAN: I think they were signaling each other.

JEFF: Oh, come on, Fran. Marsha and Dick? They wouldn't do that.

FRAN: She bids diamonds—he leads a club, and she just happens to have the ace. Things like that were happening all evening.

JEFF: Maybe they've been married so long they can read each others' minds.

FRAN: I'm serious. There were too many miraculous leads and incredible bids that just happened to fit.

JEFF: But when we play tennis with them they always lean over backward to call the balls in our favor.

FRAN: I think they have a hang-up about beating us at bridge. They can beat us at tennis without any help.

The problem of cheating and lying ranges all the way from minor everyday behavior to serious ethical decisions. If someone gives you too much change, do you return it? Why or why not?

What keeps you honest? In an analysis of all the different stages, Kohlberg says the feeling in the gut is the same at

Stage One as it is at Stage Six. But at Stage One it's the fear that you'll be punished by some outside force; at Stage Six, it's knowing you're not being true to your own principles and your conscience will make you suffer accordingly—"I'll hate myself in the morning."

To someone reasoning at an expedient Stage Two level, a good man is a boob. The husband says to his wife, who is protesting the idea of buying their son a stereo from a dubious source: "Flap your little wings, Kay, but we can get it for half the price. It's silly to pay more. Nobody really knows where the man gets them."

Moral judgment is the only *moral* factor involved in decisions like that one, but there are plenty of other factors. Opportunity, economic and social pressures, emotional problems—it's complex to relate what has been learned about cheating to stages of moral development. We can't have moral principles if we don't understand or believe in them, but we *can* possess a high level of moral judgment and not live up to it.

At the University of Chicago in 1928 and 1929, psychologists Hartshorne and May (1928–1930) conducted a series of studies on cheating in games and in the classroom and on stealing and lying. Their results challenged many of our assumptions about moral behavior and moral education. Every one of their studies led them to the same conclusion: There is no correlation between character training and behavior. Moral behavior simply isn't consistent in an individual from one situation to another. Circumstances are the most important thing—we may cheat in one situation and not in another. And there is not always a relationship between what we say about morality and what we *do*. Those people who strongly and vocally disapprove of stealing and cheating may steal and cheat as much as anyone else. Normally we all cheat a little. Think about it.

For his doctoral thesis at the University of Chicago, Richard Krebs, an associate of Kohlberg's, made a study of moral judgment and cheating (Krebs and Kohlberg, 1973). It demonstrated that such factors as will, purpose, and ego strength are involved in whether or not we cheat, along with our level of moral judgment and the pressures of the situation. Strong-willed conventional people (Stages Three and Four) apparently resist cheating more than weak-willed ones; but, surprisingly, Krebs and Kohlberg found an opposite situation at the lower stages (One and Two). There, the strong-willed cheated because they believed it would bring them an advantage, and had few scruples about it.

Even at the principled levels (Stages Five and Six), Krebs and Kohlberg found a few people who cheated, but considerably fewer—only 15 percent compared to 70 percent of the Stage One and Two people and 55 percent of Stage Three and Four subjects.

In an experiment on the effect of a moral discussion program, the subjects involved were rated at a higher level of moral development after the experiment, but there was more cheating on a test given after the discussion program than on one given before. Presumably more people cheated the second time around because the cheating on the first test was apparently undetected—they thought people had gotten away with it!

The moral thinking of our lives is often compartmentalized. We move from one area to another, from church to business, from politics to social relationships, from sports to science. For example, surveys show that many of us feel there is a gap between individual morality and political morality—we believe people use higher standards in their personal lives than they do in their political lives.

Moral independence, insistence on acting according to principles, can make you unpopular and put you in conflict with your peers, your employer, even the government. Emerson says that for nonconformity the world whips you with its displeasure; whistle blowers often pay heavily for their attempts to hold to high standards of probity.

When the West Point Academy interviewed students at random regarding the venerable honor system, Cadet Timothy Ringgold admitted to the authorities that cheating was widespread although he himself was not guilty of it. As a result he was convicted of "tolerating misconduct." According to Ringgold, "the academy was lying to perpetuate the myth that cadets don't lie, steal, or cheat. It's a very noble idea, but in any system with people there is bound to be less than perfection." Ringgold resigned, accusing the Academy of throwing out the cadets in order to keep the system, while he thought it more sensible to modify the system and work with the cadets. Although charges against him were dropped, he left the academy and enrolled at Arizona State University. After a commission investigating the cheating scandal had recommended substantial changes in the honor system, Ringgold accepted an invitation to return to West Point, along with 98 of the 152 expelled cadets.

Not only West Point has had problems with cheating and with honor systems. In a *U.S. News and World Report* article (1976), Paul Ginsberg, dean of students at the Madison campus of the University of Wisconsin, says, "What can you do about it when it is a reflection of the rest of society?" There's an apparent reluctance to report incidents of cheating, and the punishment is usually mild. Surprisingly, according to authorities, it's not the D student struggling to avoid failure who cheats, but the achiever trying for an A instead of a B. At Lehigh University, 47 percent of the students admitted they cheat sometimes; 30 percent of 2,000 Johns Hopkins University undergraduates said they had cheated during their college careers. Peer approval—whether cheating is taken seriously or condoned—does seem to make a difference, suggesting that honor systems can work if students want them to work. Most of us, however, prefer to be good fellows rather than good men or women, resent anyone who makes his or her virtue too conspicuous.

Social psychologist Jerald Jellison in *Time* magazine (1968, p. 67), states that he believes the average American tells an astounding 200 lies a day. And Sissela Bok, author of *Lying* (1978), thinks governmental lying is corrupting the whole political system; lack of veracity in all the professions is having a markedly harmful effect on society.

The Senate Governmental Affairs committee asked Robert Bloom, deputy comptroller of the currency, why he hadn't offered them full information about Bert Lance's banking record at the original hearings for Lance's confirmation (*Los Angeles Times,* Sept. 13, 1977).

"Nobody wants to be the skunk at the garden party," Bloom said. "It wasn't my responsibility to shoot down presidential appointees." He had been afraid of jeopardizing his own job as a career civil servant if he played a part in blocking Lance's nomination. "It's easy for people of independent means to be heroes," Bloom added. "I depend on my job for a living."

Bloom's comments are classic examples of the discrepancy between our moral reasoning and our behavior. Under the pressure of events, we may behave in ways typical of Stages One or Two when we have the moral comprehension of Stages Three or Four, or even higher.

And how often we pride ourselves on our own virtue when it hasn't really been tested. Dewey says we're all natural Jack Horners: "If the plum comes out when we pull out our thumb, we attribute the satisfactory result to personal virtue: 'What a good boy am I!'" But morality is a continuing process, not a fixed achievement. At every level of moral development, we all live in glass houses, our lives more transparent than we know.

Stage Five

The Social Contract
"With liberty and justice for all."

▰ **The Missing Months Dilemma** Suppose you are
Christopher Hays—a bright, articulate young man about
to graduate from New York University with a master's degree in
business administration. You are a candidate for a young executives' training program with a large corporation, and it looks as if
you will probably be accepted: Your academic record is excellent, you have a sheaf of glowing recommendations from your
professors, and your work portfolio is impressive.

But you have a serious problem to deal with on your resume:
an 18-month void between your junior and senior years at
N.Y.U. That was a terrible time in your life. You were carrying
20 units, you were working at a part-time job, and your girl-
friend broke up your relationship. All these pressures sent you
into a severe depression, and you ended up in a locked psychiatric ward.

With treatment, you slowly recovered; after a long hiatus, you
resumed your academic work, and now you have your master's
degree. Of course, you know that a thorough investigation of
your past will reveal the 18-month gap, and you'll have to account for it somehow in interviews and on employment applications. You also know that your true medical history will hinder
your chances of being hired by the conservative company now

considering you for their training program, which in most cases leads to the higher echelons of management.

You could lie and say that you took a leave of absence during those months, that you went home to Michigan because of family problems. Or perhaps you could juggle the dates on your resume and cover the gap that way. You feel fine, by the way. Your confidence in yourself is entirely restored and your doctor assures you that he sees little likelihood of a recurrence.

What should you do? Why?

(See page 88 for a discussion of options.)

When you move beyond the conventional levels, Stages Three and Four, to the postconventional stages, Five and Six, you've taken a giant step. Moral judgment now rests on principles that you've chosen for yourself. Stage Five reasoning is organized around a social contract: How to make laws that will guarantee the rights of everyone, because individual rights are as important as the welfare of the group. There's a striving for a reasoned, rational perspective—if you're to be a part of a society, then the structure of that society must make sense to you; you must be able to view it as upholding inviolable rights. It must recognize and protect those rights. At this stage, life has a greater value than property. At this level, the answer to the question "When is it appropriate to break a law?" is determined by principles of justice and fairness.

Our friend Mark, now 20, gives a Stage Five response to the problem of the Captain and the Troublemaker: "According to the rules of the army," he says, "a soldier can't refuse an order like that; but as a human being the Troublemaker has the right to refuse. When a man enters the army, it is understood that there are going to be risks, but he hasn't agreed to commit suicide."

In his famous essay on self-reliance ([1841] 1926) Emerson wrote, "Nothing can bring you peace but yourself. Nothing can bring you peace but the triumph of principles. . . . Whoever would be a man must be a nonconformist, unhindered by the name of goodness, exploring for himself whether or not it is goodness." Morality at Stages Five and Six is keyed to universal human rights, to principles rather than to the rules and conventions of society. Stage Five reasoning accepts laws because of the social contract, the necessity for agreement among people living together.

But there are some laws and rules to which we, as reasonable people, can't be expected to commit ourselves; these we should challenge. There are basic human rights, minimum guarantees that any society must make to its members in order for them to believe that their commitment to that society makes sense in ethical terms.

Dewey describes the difference between Stage Four and Stage Five as a movememt from custom to conscience, from group morality to personal morality. This is a big step, and one that most of us haven't taken yet. It's here that we begin to see individuals challenging authority, questioning whether a law is just or unjust.

At four in the morning, in Paris, a taxi driver came to a red light, stopped, looked in every direction, and drove on through the deserted intersection. His American passenger was shocked, and asked him why he hadn't waited for the light. "Because, monsieur," the driver said, "I am a man with a brain, I am not a machine. I can see that there is no person, no vehicle, not even a cat, approaching in any direction, and I see no reason to sit here mindlessly waiting for the light to change, wasting my time and yours." He had chosen to disobey a law—not an unjust law but one that, at the moment, he thought it foolish and unnecessary to obey.

At Stage Five, there are collisions between the interests of the group and the independent beliefs of the individual. The clashes are between order and progress, between the strong, conforming bonds of habit and the effort to think for oneself, to opt for reform or to seek out new ways of viewing moral issues. We move to higher levels of judgment only when we choose our own principles rather than accept ready-made opinions, when we become aware of our almost unconscious identification with the group that has habitually directed our thinking.

Dewey said that conflict is the gadfly of thought. Experiences that sting us into questioning and commitment seem necessary if we are to move from the conventional stages (Three and Four) to principled levels of thinking (Five and Six). We must pass through the fire of conflict and problem solving in order to change our perspective. Responsibility alone won't do it—most adults have experience of responsibility, yet most never reach the highest stages of moral judgment. For some, however, confrontation and change provide the stimulus that leads to an understanding of higher moral reasoning. We need challenges to our conventional ideas to be shocked into the levels of thinking that are essential for moral growth.

At the highest levels of reasoning, moral principles define what is right for anyone in any situation. The Golden Rule is such a principle, demanding that you treat others as you would wish to be treated. Another is Kant's categorical imperative.

At Stage Five, our riotous friend Derek would decide on a time to end his noisy party by considering what would be best for all the tenants in the building. He would probably have worked out rules as to reasonable times for the close of such celebrations, taking everyone's wishes fairly into account, and these rules would have been informed by strongly held principles.

Principles are in contrast at this stage to specific sets of rules such as the Ten Commandments or to the more restricted rules of conventional behavior that might determine, for example, what would be right for a Democrat but not for a Republican, or for an American but not for a Russian.

A family reasoning at Stage Five can serve as a microcosm of the larger social contract. Andrew and Catherine Greenhalt are both professors at a large state university in the South. They adjust their lives to differing family needs. When Catherine had the babies, she stayed home; when it was feasible, she began to work alternately with Andrew at the university, and he shared the household tasks. The Greenhalts look on their marriage as a contract designed to meet the emotional, financial, and social needs of all the family members, each one considered an equally important part of the whole. The family contract takes in the reciprocity of Stage Two, the love and concern of Stage Three, and the responsibility to the larger social order of Stage Four.

The Greenhalt children, Karin and Tommy, take their share of responsibility. They raise a little hell but are mostly a delight to their parents. They're old enough now that Andrew and Catherine can handle discipline with a reasoning process. When the children were very little, there were rules they had to obey—such as not running in front of cars—but now the rules are the result of joint discussion and accommodation. Of course, there are problems—whose turn it is to wash the dog; forgotten or avoided chores, staying out late with friends without calling home—but these problems are talked out, with lots of argument and very little shouting.

With a chance to involve themselves in their own upbringing, Karin and Tommy are enabled to understand what's fair and what's best for their family, and they have a reason to live up to what is agreed on and what is expected of them. Rebellion is defused because it would be rebellion against themselves, against concepts and processes that they helped work out. The rule in family discussions is that whenever there is disagreement each person must state the opposing positions in order to show that he or she understands them and has some concept of what it would mean to occupy that position him- or herself.

Last week, for instance, Tommy was half an hour late bringing his mother's car home, because he had helped out a friend who needed a ride. As a consequence, Catherine was late for an important appointment. The family talked it out and agreed that, in future, having the car back on time would take precedence even over a friend's needs—unless Tommy called first to see if the time could be extended. Catherine appreciated Tommy's wish to help his friend. In his turn, Tommy realized that "it was a bummer to make her so late for her appointment."

At Stage Five, "right" is defined by the idea that, by living in society, we've made a commitment to respect and uphold the rights of others. Morality is the maintenance of that social contract, the obligation to society. According to this reasoning, basic values such as life and liberty must be maintained even when they conflict with existing laws. Laws are obeyed, but not blindly; we see human rights as more important than the rigid enforcement of existing codes. The structure of society is important because it upholds the rights and the welfare of its individual members.

When is it right for us as individuals to become involved with the law, to try to prevent a crime or to intervene in a police process? Betty Smith and her husband were sitting in a movie theater, watching the latest Pink Panther film, laughing uproariously at the performance of Peter Sellers as the bumbling Inspector Clouzot. Suddenly a male voice in the audience shouted, "Stop it! Cut it out!" There were sounds of a scuffle, of blows being struck. Another voice muttered something about a name. "So I called you a name?" shouted the first voice. "Is that any reason to hit me?" There was a heavier thud.

"Stop it!" cried the first voice. "You broke my glasses. I'm bleeding! Look, everybody, look! He's using a club! Look at him!"

The audience sat silent. The laughter had stopped. Confused as to just what was happening, Betty felt her stomach heave—there was no doubt that one man was severely beating another as they moved along a row and up the side aisle of the theater. Without any conscious reflection, Betty was surprised to hear herself shout, "Stop it! Let him alone!"

In that moment, as though a spell had been broken by Betty's intervention, a dozen men, including her husband, jumped up and ran toward the rear of the theater, where the two men were still scuffling. Police arrived, ushers joined them to isolate the combatants, and the violence stopped. The man who'd shouted was indeed bleeding, his broken glasses askew on his face. From the surface evidence, Betty and her husband theorized that the attacker must have been a plain-clothes vice officer and that his victim was a homosexual who'd been entrapped; such incidents were common at that time in Betty's town. But she and her husband never did learn what it had all been about, nor did they ever see anything reported in the papers.

Still, Betty felt good about her small role in speaking out. She was glad that she'd gone against her strong urge to mind her own business and let the police or the theater employees take care of the matter. Such thoughts, she knew, hold us immobilized in times when we should act. But she didn't feel like a heroine. In the darkness and anonymity of the theater, it had been easy enough to shout. But what if she'd been walking down a street alone and had encountered a similar situation? It's hard to take action, whatever your level of moral judgment, when you're outnumbered or when the assailant is armed or larger and stronger than you are. Stage Five reasoning is concerned with all the individuals in a society, defining them all as neighbors toward whom we have responsibility. But many people who want to follow the impulse to *act* at that level have deliberately taken up the study of the martial arts in order to ensure that their interventions will not end in disaster.

There is some connection here with the founding fathers of the United States, who not only wrote and signed their names to documents of revolutionary significance in the history of man's freedoms but also were resolved to defend their views with all their resources. Their Constitution is regarded by Kohlberg as a Stage Five document. In a paper titled "The Lessons of Watergate" (1974, p. 1), Kohlberg notes that, "by some uncanny wisdom, some eighteenth-century gentlemen farmers with a prescientific understanding of human nature and of society devised a document called the Constitution. This was the first document in history to establish government on the basis of what I call principled morality, a Stage Five set of postulated universal rights of man and a conception of a government as a social contract *freely chosen* and designed to protect the rights of all individuals who were party to the contract."

From this perspective, the great tragedy of Watergate was that Nixon and most of his associates apparently reasoned at a conventional, conforming Stage Three or Four level, sometimes even oriented just to the simple reciprocity of Stage Two: "You'd better take care of me, after all the favors I've done for you." In his book *Plain Speaking* (1973), Merle Miller reports Harry Truman's opinion that Nixon didn't really understand the Constitution or its power to uphold individual rights. Nor did Nixon seem to understand the Stage Five reasoning of many of the men who opposed him—Ervin, Baker, Cox, Richardson—men who were striving to be fair and principled.

Most of us reason at the Stage Four, law-and-order level, and many of us orginally supported the justification that anything can be excused if you identify those whose rights you violate as enemies of the state. Gradually, however, the public began to see the Watergate confrontation as a battle between people acting in an unprincipled, self-serving way and opponents acting in the name of justice for the protection of individual rights. It was reassuring to see the Constitution at the heart of a modern morality play, guaranteeing that no one is above the law and that justice can triumph.

Because the Constitution is a truly principled document, it works even when those heading the government are unprincipled. Because it is venerated, it is upheld even by an electorate that doesn't always fully understand it.

Every few years, the Gallup Poll takes an opinion survey of the Bill of Rights without identifying it by name. Each time, vast numbers of people surveyed are shocked at its provisions and reject its guarantees as dangerously radical. Under the U.S. Constitution, our rights receive greater protection than many are willing to grant to others on a universal basis.

The American Civil Liberties Union (ACLU) was founded to protect the right of freedom of speech, and the other freedoms spelled out in the Constitution, for everyone—particularly those involved with unpopular causes; even the repulsive, the disliked, the outrageous. In the tradition of Voltaire, the ACLU is dedicated to defend to the death anyone's right to say anything. In the process, it has offended a great many people. Long identified with the defense of minority rights, the ACLU lost almost a quarter of its membership in 1977 and 1978 when it decided to support the First Amendment rights of a small group of American Nazis in Skokie, Illinois. Skokie is predominantly Jewish, and its population includes a number of concentration camp survivors. When the Nazis sought a permit to parade there, the city fathers responded by obtaining a court order banning the rally. But the people of Skokie did more than that. They passed laws giving their officials the power to deny a permit to anyone to speak, parade or demonstrate if, in the opinion of the officials, the proposed activity portrayed a "lack of virtue" in others or incited hostility. The ACLU saw those laws as unconstitutional and argued that they could set a dangerous precedent, enabling communities everywhere to forbid any speech they might decide was offensive.

In the past few years, the ACLU had become associated with such "liberal" causes as ending the Vietnam War and the impeachment of President Nixon. In these efforts, it had acquired many members who were perhaps not in sympathy with the fundamental reasons for the organization's existence. These members were startled to learn that the First Amendment protects not only *their* rights and the rights of those whose ideas they support or tolerate but also the rights of those with whom they vehemently disagree—even those

81

whose arguments display a "lack of virtue," as in the Skokie ordinance.

This is a difficult concept for all of us reasoning below the level of Stage Five—in other words, the great majority. We may wonder what these civil liberties are, anyway. How would parents who lost a son fighting against Nazi Germany in World War II feel about this business? Does it make any sense to them to ask a court to protect the right of a handful of native Nazis to parade in a Jewish community? Does it make any sense to help people with warped ideas to perpetuate a set of beliefs that nearly everyone finds morally outrageous? And, while we're at it, isn't it morally wrong to put the snowy white blanket of the First Amendment over the obscenities of Larry Flynt's *Hustler* Magazine?

Unfortunately for this level of reasoning, there are no boundaries to the First Amendment. U.S. Supreme Court Justice Black, in a 1962 interview emphasized that when the Constitution said, "Congress shall make no law respecting an establishment of religion, or prohibiting the free exercise thereof; or abridging the freedom of speech, or of the press," it means exactly that. No law.

It is this concern for the minority's rights of speech and assembly that primarily distinguishes the concept of law and order from that of justice. A Supreme Court decision in the case of *West Virginia Board of Education* v. *Barnette,* in 1943, says it superbly: "Freedom to differ is not limited to things that do not matter much. That would be a mere shadow of freedom. The test of its substance is the right to differ as to things that touch the heart of the existing order.

"If there is any fixed star in our constitutional constellation, it is that no official, high or petty, can prescribe what shall be orthodox in politics, nationalism, religion, or other matters of opinion or force citizens to confess by word or act their faith therein. If there are any circumstances which permit an exception, they do not now occur to us."

At conventional stages Three and Four, reasoning is strongly oriented to conformity, both by those in authority and by the rank and file. But at Stage Five, concern with the obligations of membership in the society involves the willingness to challenge existing laws and methods, to question authority and the status quo if it seems a necessary means to finding the solution to social problems.

From a Stage Four perspective, there is no way to change the society; at Stage Five, we realize that it *can* be changed and that we don't have to keep on doing things the same way. All very well as theory, of course—but it's not always simple to put into practice. The courage to act is as important as the level of our moral judgment.

As Harry Truman told Merle Miller (in Miller, 1973) it's not so hard to know the right thing to do; the problem is doing it. The challenge is to find bravery equal to our level of moral understanding. It's no easy thing to go against family, friends, neighbors, in order to stand for unpopular or unconventional beliefs. It takes guts. But it's the only way to bring about the changes we desire.

The possibility of taking action with Stage Five reasoning can crop up even in an apparently impossible situation. Consider the case of Michael Bernhardt, an American soldier in Vietnam who refused an order to fire at Vietnamese civilians. After a reprimand from his commanding officer, Bernhardt decided for himself that in future he would fire and miss. Realizing that he couldn't change the attitude of those in command, he decided simply to bypass them. "I am going to be doing my own war and let them do *their* own war."

Unlike other soldiers in the same situation who willingly obeyed orders, Bernhardt had his own strong principles. He didn't believe in killing civilians. He upheld everyone's right to life. In his view, the civilian woman he was ordered to shoot "was in her own country. . . . There was nothing to indicate that she was anything but what she appeared to

83

be . . . a noncombatant." So, when he was given the order to fire, he disobeyed it—a highly unorthodox procedure for a soldier.

The unorthodox is rarely encountered because of the power of orthodoxy in all areas of life, particularly in the professions. Doing things as they have always been done hampers even medical research, as Albert Szent-Gyorgyi, a Nobel Prize winner for his discovery of Vitamin C, pointed out in an insert written for *Executive Health* in February, 1978. Szent-Gyorgyi says that we don't understand cancer any better today than Rudolph Virchow did a hundred years ago. Virchow is considered the father of modern pathology, and originated the phrase "every cell from a cell"—all living things come from other living things. Szent-Gyorgyi notes that the astounding progress of medical science in the last century has largely bypassed the degenerative diseases. He argues that an explanation of cancer must be sought in the subatomic dimension, in basic cell research apart from the "targeted" cancer projects favored by the establishment and thus subsidized by public and private grants.

But Szent-Gyorgyi (1978) says that the committees distributing research grants have a distaste for new ideas. Cancer research, he points out, demands people with intuition and the daring to go after new approaches. Szent-Gyorgyi says that if Louis Pasteur should arise from his grave and want to go to work on the problem, he wouldn't have much of a chance. In his article, the doctor gives us an imaginary dialogue between Pasteur and a representative of the National Institute of Health (NIH):

PASTEUR: I would like to work on cancer, and I need a grant.

NIH: You have only to write down exactly what you will do and why.

PASTEUR: Research is going out into the unknown, and I don't know what I will find and do there.

NIH: How do you expect us to waste money on you if you do not

know yourself what you will do? We are responsible for the taxpayers' money and have to know what will be done with it.
PASTEUR: Thank you. I left my grave open, and I'm going back.

Another medical expert who looks at old problems in new ways is Doctor Oliver Cope, professor emeritus of surgery at Harvard Medical School. "Your care is in your own hands," says Dr. Cope. "You should question the way society treats you and challenge whatever seems wrong." Although Dr. Cope has treated hundreds of breast cancer patients, he has not performed a mastectomy since 1960. According to him, when the cancer is still localized, a mastectomy is not indicated; a much simpler operation is sufficient. And if the cancer has already spread, then even a radical mastectomy won't get rid of wandering malignant cells. Cope's approach is to employ surgery to remove the malignancy and a limited amount of surrounding tissue, followed by radiotherapy or chemotherapy, depending on the type of cancer and the size of the tumor. While Cope's results and other studies over the past nearly 20 years indicate that radical procedures in breast cancer are in most cases not necessary, most members of the medical establishment continue to perform the same type of operation first done 80 years ago. Meanwhile, the public mind has made near-heroines of women thus mutilated.

However, cracks do seem to be appearing in the white-tiled walls of the medical establishment. There are many doctors, researchers, and patients all working to temper the heavy weight of Stage Four orthodoxy with Stage Five curiosity and concern. There is a new willingness to consider new ideas and to give them complete examination, so that if they are rejected it will be on the ground of proof rather than prejudice.

Just one man with a social conscience *can* make an impact. Consider the story of Jean Henri Dunant, founder of the International Red Cross. Dunant, a Swiss, was on tour in Italy in 1859, when France attacked Austria. He watched the battle of Solferino from a hilltop and saw thousands of dead and wounded men lying on the battlefield after the conflict. Dunant was appalled at their suffering and at the absence of any medical care for them, and—unorthodoxly—decided to try to do something about it.

He managed to approach the French emperor and talked him into releasing captured Austrian doctors to tend the wounded. He also organized residents of the vicinity to help. And he published a pamphlet about his experiences, asking, "Would it not be possible to found and organize in all civilized countries permanent societies of volunteers who in time of war would give help to the wounded without regard for their nationality?" It was possible: Dunant's idea led to the Geneva conference and the Red Cross Society. Treaties were signed that provided for the humane treatment of wounded men and prisoners of war, and guaranteed the protection of civilian populations in wartime.

This kind of action, by individuals who reason at Stages Five and Six, who do not accept injustice and do not think that human suffering is inevitable, and who have the courage of their beliefs, can change the world—and often has. And, while the conditions that Dunant fought against still persist, they are no longer ignored or taken for granted.

There is a good example of social contract consciousness in San Francisco today, in the functioning of seven mediation boards in the Visitacion Valley Neighborhood Community. In this highly unconventional approach to problems of law, order and neighborhood security, residents themselves sit on boards to resolve problems of minor crime, neighborhood disputes and complaints, petty thefts, landlord-tenant issues, the neighbor with too many dogs—the sort of thing often dismissed or plea-bargained out of court.

For example, Asian owners of a local grocery caught a 12-year-old boy robbing their store. They didn't want to call the police because the boy was so young; additionally, he was black, and they were afraid of antagonizing the black community. The case was handled by one of the boards, which didn't try to determine guilt or innocence but sought to help the people involved to define exactly what happened and to find a solution that satisfied both sides.

In another instance, a group of teenagers broke into a local house and were identified by neighbors. At a board hearing, the teenagers talked about why they had done it, and the owner talked about the betrayal he felt in knowing that children in his own neighborhood would want to rob him. After a thorough airing of everyone's feelings, the teenagers agreed to do a minimum of 20 hours of work in community jobs as a concrete and positive reparation for their act and to contribute something affirmative to their neighborhood.

Another instance of concern for the social contract is the privately funded Westside Fair Housing Council of Los Angeles. This organization works to ensure implementation of the Fair Housing Law, which provides that all U.S. citizens have the right to buy a house or to rent an apartment without regard to race or color. The trick, of course, is to translate that right into action; when that is impossible, the Westside Council intervenes. For example, Shelley is a young black woman who is an executive secretary. When she went to rent an attractive apartment, the manager told her to return on the following Monday. On Monday, he told her that the apartment had been rented. Shelley told her boss about this and about how disappointed she was. Shelley thought it was just bad luck, but her boss was skeptical. He called the manager and discovered that the apartment was still available—to him. The Westside Council was called in, conciliation was arranged, and Shelley got her apartment.

This is a happy ending to a sad situation. Even with fair laws on the books, the society remains in need of organizations of this kind—organizations with a Stage Five perspective, concerned with fairness and equality for all members of society—to keep prodding away at all of us and at the patterns of thinking that have held us for so long.

Today there is scarcely an injustice anywhere on earth that

doesn't have individuals or an organization working against it. Most of these combatants have goals that are informed by principled Stage Five reasoning. They seek justice for the deprived and disadvantaged, and work to overcome the inequities that exist in every society. Even when the organization is primarily a money-making one—and there are still plenty of these, designed to benefit their officers in a self-serving, Stage Two fashion—a Stage Five appeal for money is invariably used. Letters and pamphlets speak to our conscience, asking for help to achieve social or legal or economic justice for those who may have slipped through the mesh of Stage Four law and order or who somehow got left behind in a Stage Two scramble for subsistence.

Levels of moral reasoning, of course, mix and blend not only in organizations but also in each of us individually. But the more we examine our own actions and motives, the closer we can come to a merger of the highest level of moral judgment of which we are capable with what we actually *do* when confronted with hard choices. It is perhaps not given to many of us to be Dunants, but it *is* possible to integrate our best thinking with the daily living of our lives.

◥ **THE MISSING MONTHS DILEMMA—A DISCUSSION OF OPTIONS** With Stage One reasoning, you'd decide to tell the truth because if you lied you might get caught and lose your chance for the program anyway.

If you decided that it's your right to keep the matter confidential, that you qualify in every way for the opening and see no reason to mention your mental breakdown on the application form, you'd be reasoning at Stage Two.

At Stage Three, wanting to be seen as the perfect choice, you'd think it foolish to spoil the "bright young man on his way up" picture of yourself by confessing a weakness such as a serious mental breakdown. You won't mention it on the application but will use the family problems story if asked to explain the gap on your resume.

At Stage Four, you decide to mention the matter briefly because the rules require that you give a complete history and you feel you must follow the correct procedure.

Using the social contract reasoning at Stage Five, you decide that you have an obligation to be honest and give all the relevant facts that are requested. You explain what happened and describe your doctor's opinion that recurrence is unlikely. You'll rely on your good record and qualifications to get you your chance.

Stage Six

Universal Human Rights
"With malice toward none."

■ **The Prisoners' Dilemma** Suppose you are one of three prisoners in the hospital compound of a prisoner-of-war camp. All three of you are suffering from an illness that requires special medication each day to keep you alive. Through the usually reliable grapevine, word reaches you that rescuing forces are only three days away. Most of the camp personnel have fled, but you are too weak to flee the camp. You have only enough medication for one person for three days; there's no way to obtain more medicine.

What would you do? Why?

(See page 100 for a discussion of options.)

The power of thought, the potential of reason, is universal among mankind. It follows that this reason speaks no less universally to us all with its "Thou Shalts." There is then world law, we are all fellow citizens and the world is a single city. Is there any other citizenship that can be claimed by all humanity?

Marcus Aurelius, *Meditations*

Stage Six reasoning is based on the concept of justice, on universal, unchanging principles that apply to anyone in any situation. Every man and woman has the same rights, every individual has a claim on freedom and human dignity that is as valid as the claim of any other. Stage Six is identified with philosophical concepts rarely seen in studies of the stages of moral development. Few people are classified at this level, and some stage development psychologists question whether Stage Six even exists separately from Stage Five. We will describe it as it appears in much of the work of Kohlberg and his associates.

A fully matured Mark, at Stage Six, again comments on the Captain's dilemma: "It's unfair to single out anyone to go, since any human life has the same value. But if someone must go, it should not be based on saying what his life is worth. As a matter of principle, you have to look on every life as sacred. If the Troublemaker can do the job best, then he should go, but not because his life is less important. Even the Troublemaker sees that the Captain was forced by his concern for the lives of all to choose one life."

At this level, we seek agreement on a set of ideal principles that would be valid apart from the civic order; principles that all of us, all men and women, could agree to and act on in our own dealings with one another—in other words, ultimate moral values, including the inviolate value of human life.

People who reason at Stage Six are often in conflict with the fixed rules and conventions of law-and-order societies. Because they see everyone's rights as equally important and regard all individuals as ends, not means, they are sometimes viewed as revolutionaries, rabble-rousers seeking to stir up trouble. They afflict the comfortable as they comfort the afflicted, and they are not always welcomed or even tolerated by the political or religious establishment. Caught in a conflict between differing concepts of law and justice, they are often far ahead of the thinking of their own time. Often they are misunderstood, abused, and vilified, sometimes put to death. Jesus Christ, the most obvious example, was in constant trouble with the authorities for preaching a simple doctrine of love and forgiveness. In the climate of that time, he was seen as a dangerous threat to the establishment.

Mohandas Gandhi dedicated himself to his people's welfare for over half a century, and took to the humble dress of the dhoti and walking stick, symbolic of poor pilgrims, in a conscious effort to identify himself with those at the bottom of the social order. He had read the *Bhagavad-Gita* at the age of 20 and was struck by its teaching that a man's holy duty was to struggle in the world without regard for the consequences. Saints and moral heroes are those who take literally the homilies that the rest of us merely quote and admire. While most of us would be embarrassed to practice these moral injunctions in our daily lives, would feel silly or ridiculous to do so, some few do not equivocate, and express their moral judgment in everything they do.

Martin Luther King adopted Gandhi's methods in his own struggle against injustice and racial discrimination. He believed that nonviolent resistance was a powerful weapon. Early in his career, he told his followers, "If you will protest courageously, and yet with dignity and Christian love, when the history books are written in future generations the historians will have to pause and say, 'There lived a great people—a black people—who injected new meaning and dignity into the veins of civilization' " (Miller, p. 40).

Perhaps more eloquently than anyone of his era, King clarified the ways in which principles of justice can conflict with civil law. In his "Letter from a Birmingham Jail," he wrote, "One may well ask, 'How can you advocate breaking some laws and obeying others?' The answer lies in the fact that one has not only a legal but a moral responsibility to obey just laws. One has a moral responsibility to disobey unjust laws, though one must do so openly, lovingly and with a willingness to accept the penalty. An individual who breaks a law that conscience tells him is unjust, and accepts the penalty to arouse the conscience of the community, is expressing in reality the highest respect for law. An unjust law is a human law not rooted in eternal law and natural law. A law that uplifts human personality is just, one which degrades human personality is unjust" (King, p. 85).

Stage Six is the level of reasoning that characterizes moral heroes, and social observers have complained that our own era suffers from a lack of such heroes. For a *Saturday Review* article in 1976, John Neary made a personal survey of friends, acquaintances, scholars, scientists, druggists, whomever he met on a cross-country trip, asking each to name "the greatest living American." Invariably, each person was a bit startled, and most couldn't come up with anybody they could wholeheartedly qualify as "great."

Who, these days, is a contemporary hero to you? It isn't easy to find or to define such people. In contemporary America, it seems to require a public relations firm to create a certified hero. "We're in times that discourage hero creation," says Columbia University professor Charles Frankel, president of the National Humanities Center. "It's a marketing economy. We market products, and to some extent we market people. There is a forced obsolescence involved.

"The age of the celebrity is hurting the hero. . . . A democracy rests on the power of ordinary people to achieve eminence and distinction; the quality of a democracy rests on the quality of its heroes" (*Los Angeles Times*, May 24, 1978).

James Epperson, associate professor of English at Dartmouth College, held a seminar called, "Where Have All the Heroes Gone?" Epperson feels it may be that the social conditions at the end of the twentieth century make heroism impossible. At the very least, the role is a dangerous one. Even in the best of times, it takes courage to speak out on behalf of the disenfranchised, the oppressed; popularity never lies that way. In decades that are clearly not the best, the social reformer risks not only the repudiations of a scorning majority but also the violent backlash that is the signature of our times.

Yet apparently we still feel the need for heroes, preferably live ones. They give us patterns of noble behavior, stimulate our own capacity for greatness, and make us proud of our society. But how many of us are moved by the list of admired people finally gathered by Neary for that piece in *Saturday Review* and offered with a sense of embarrassment and inadequacy: Teddy Kennedy, George Wallace, Margaret Mead, Wernher von Braun, O. J. Simpson, Leon Jaworski, Ralph Nader, and Bobby Fischer?

One figure who has attracted worldwide admiration is Mother Teresa, the Yugoslavian nun who has labored more than 30 years among the abject poor—the scabrously diseased and dying—of Calcutta, in the course of her work founding the Roman Catholic Missionaries of Charity, who now number nearly 1,300 nuns and brothers. These missionaries, who allow to themselves no more than the poor among whom they work, are now scattered throughout 37 countries, including the United States—where they can be found in New York City's South Bronx and in the slum streets of Los Angeles.

Sister Teresa and her followers do not proselytize. They simply tend "the poorest of the poor," to live out, as she says, "that life of love, of compassion, that God has for his people." Mother Teresa has said (*Time* magazine, 1976, p. 54) that the poor suffer more from rejection than from material want. "If we didn't discard them," she says, "they would not be poor. Loneliness and the feeling of being unwanted is the most terrible poverty."

It is Teresa's understanding of that, her empathy extended in a real identification with those whom most of us reject, that most clearly exemplifies Stage Six reasoning—at which plateau of consciousness the rights of others are not only equal to one's own but even, in a spirit of true selflessness, more important than one's own. It is no very great surprise to us that figures of such heroic stature are as rare as hen's teeth—in this society or in any earlier one.

There is a similar if less extreme example in the efforts of two women in northern Ireland to end the long tradition of violence there between Catholics and Protestants. In 1977,

Betty Williams and Mairead Corrigan, two Catholic women from Belfast, received a special Norwegian "People's Peace Prize" as well as the Nobel Peace Prize for their courage in speaking out against prejudice and killing.

It began when Mairead Corrigan's niece and two nephews—Joann, eight years; John, two years; and Andrew, six weeks—were struck and killed on a Belfast street by a car out of control; the driver, an Irish Republican Army (IRA) man, had been shot to death by a British soldier. Somehow the senseless deaths, added to the thousands of others in northern Ireland, marshaled Corrigan and her friend Betty Williams to do something about the appalling toll in human lives and values.

They quietly organized a peaceful demonstration that drew 10,000 participants from both Protestant and Catholic districts. People long regarded as irreconcilable enemies came together. The two women simply ignored the verbal abuse, the obscene letters, the threats and slogans appearing on the streets—"Death to Betty Williams," for example—and have pressed on with their work of reconciliation as their only possible option in such dreadful times. Williams has said that part of the prize money will go toward making one of her dreams come true. "I would like to see a massive recreation center here in Belfast," she says. "I feel our children have lost the art of playing, and I would love to give it back to them" (*Los Angeles Times*, Oct. 11, 1977).

On a recent visit to America, Corrigan explained that she and Williams see their movement as an alternative to the present political system, a model of nonviolent community democracy as opposed to a situation that is divisive and sectarian, in which people vote not on the basis of issues but rather on religious affiliation.

And she sees the walls coming down. "I think now we have come to respect each other and approach each other with a sense of sharing," she said. "I think we insult people when we try to make them accept our religion or our political ideologies or our cultures. We've got to give them our time, to give them our love, to give them our concern, and ask nothing in return" (*Los Angeles Times*, March 26, 1978).

Such selflessness sometimes compels one to work outside the system. Desmond Wilson, a rebel citizen-priest in Northern Ireland, working independently in the poor Belfast neighborhood, deliberately left the shelter of religion in order to pursue the struggle for peace. As he explained to a reporter in March of 1978, "I was afraid that if I stayed [in the church] another year, what little courage I had would be gone. That's one thing that institutions do; they sap the courage. You see men you respect who refuse to act because of fear. It's like the royal favor at court. I was afraid of becoming a compliant, complacent member of the system, so I fled" (*US*, p. 32).

Wilson is one of the few people in Ulster who can talk to terrorists on both sides, and he believes that they have a sincere desire to find a way beyond violence. "These are not bad people fighting each other," he says. "They are good people fighting each other. That's the sad thing . . . when they're so full of goodness" (p. 33).

Again we see empathy in action—a projection of the self to others, an identification made with principles of universal goodness—the kind of leap that most of us cannot make, or are afraid to, fearing, as rational people must, the threats and dangers and serious sacrifices that come with such moral leaps. The best most of us can aspire to is that stage of reasoning that permits us to encourage the works of groups genuinely concerned with universal human rights. One of these, Amnesty International (AI), gives more than lip service to the plight of those suffering unjustly for their beliefs.

In every issue of *Matchbox*, the quarterly publication of Amnesty International, the following vignette appears: "During the final days of World War II, a captured resistance member sat alone in the dark of a prison cell, tired and hungry, convinced of approaching death. After weeks of torture and torment, the prisoner was sure there was no hope, no one knew or cared. But in the middle of the night the door of the cell opened and the jailer, shouting abuse into the darkness, threw a loaf of bread on the dirt floor. The prisoner tore open the loaf. Inside was a matchbox. Inside this matchbox, there were matches and a strip of paper. He lit a match. On the paper there was a single word: 'Corragio!' Take courage. Don't give up, don't give in. We are trying to help you. 'Corragio!' "

Since its founding in 1961, by London lawyer Peter Benenson, AI has sought to send such a message by various means to political prisoners all over the world. Meanwhile, AI has helped to secure the release of more than 13,000 of these "prisoners of conscience." AI wants it known that people in the world do care, and that injustice, mass arrests, mock trials, and torture are not just news items.

The United Nations International Declaration of Human Rights, adopted in 1948, is a noble document, largely unimplemented. Meanwhile, AI volunteers have become remarkably effective pitting their moral force against national power. The organization is privately funded and independent of any government, political party, ideology, or religion. In 1977, the group was awarded the Nobel Peace Prize. It has enrolled over 70,000 members in 62 countries; their work is typical of behavior motivated by Stage Five and Six reasoning and is based on a concern for the rights of minorities and the protection of human dignity.

Membership consists both of professional volunteers—lawyers, diplomats, researchers—and laypeople. AI's secretariat in London secures news about arrests, investigates cases of people in prison, and follows the political and legal activities in over a hundred countries. In special situations, leading jurists or diplomats are dispatched to attend controversial trials or to plead for the lives of those under sentence of death. With chapters throughout the world, AI has been granted consultative status to the United Nations, the Organization of American States, the Council of Europe, and the Organization of

African Unity. AI conducts investigations of torture and persecution in dozens of countries and publishes its findings, which are considered remarkably reliable in an area where information is obviously hard to come by.

Typical of Amnesty International's network of volunteers is Group 17 in Great Neck, New York. Since 1972, this group has helped to secure the release of prisoners from the Sudan, Ghana, Rhodesia, Chile, and India. Thirteen regular members, including a guidance counselor, a librarian, a lawyer, a journalist, a social worker, a housewife and a law student, meet once a month to organize activities on behalf of specific prisoners, and to assess and divide the work. Letters are carefully and courteously worded; it's not invective that gets the results, but persistence, together with the weapon of publicity.

Group 17 works continuously on behalf of its adopted prisoners. For example, there is Mark Nashpits of the Soviet Union, a dentist in his middle twenties who was sentenced to five years in Siberian exile for "disturbing public order" during a minor demonstration for the right of Soviet Jews to emigrate. The group has sent Mark a quantity of postcards, letters, and packages. Mark wrote to one member, "Everybody asks what do I need and what can they send me. I need freedom" (*Matchbox*, p. 9).

Exactly. With their letters to the authorities, with their persistence, the group was able to obtain freedom for Claudio Hector Alemany Gonzales in Chile. He wrote, "I was one of those people you worked for in such a dignified and intense way that the steel walls of the concentration camps did open up. . . . I believe that what you did for me was a real victory" (*Matchbox*, p. 9).

A truly universal concern with justice, typical of Stage Six reasoning, obliges us to feel the same outrage at violations of civil or human rights in our own country that we sense when we read about such violations abroad. It's easy to bristle with indignation at what the Soviets did, or the South Africans, or the Chileans, or the Irish. But when the prisoners are native Americans and Amnesty International is concerned, what's the reaction? "Why are *they* sticking their noses into our business when we have constitutional guarantees against such things? *We* have no concentration camps, no Gestapo or NKVD!" Do we say that? Not at Stage Six, where it's an aspect of principled thinking to recognize injustice even when it's laid at our own door.

Somewhat similar to Stage Six reasoning is the guiding philosophy of the Quakers, the Society of Friends, which is dependent on the triumph of principles, conforming not to the world but rather to an inner "light." While Quaker motivation is characterized by a search for the spirit of God within each of us, it is based neither on formal religious principles nor on dogma. Quakers accept that there is some variation in the degree of truth perceptible to each person. They hold that the whole truth is accessible to each person who continues to seek it but that some people apprehend more of it more readily than others.

For example, since the society's origin in the seventeenth century, Quakers have opposed participation in war. But if a man's conscience urges him to fight, they believe that he must follow that principle. If he continues to strive to experience more of the "light," they believe that eventually he will come to see the error in all fighting. According to the Quakers, in the first instance he would be a coward if he did not fight; in the second, a coward if he did.

The Society of Friends is made up of admittedly imperfect individuals who seek the truth from within, in a tradition of personal moral reasoning. For 300 years, they have been active in the cause of the oppressed and the exploited. They take unpopular positions, fight losing battles and walk into the lion's mouth—for justice, which to them expresses the will of God. They have consistently supported civil liberties and have been prepared to use civil disobedience when they believed it to be an instrument of justice. Typical was the refusal of two Quaker ladies to take an anticommunist oath in Maryland under the Ober Law. They refused not because they were communists but because they opposed witch hunts and oaths.

A Baltimore newspaper ran the sarcastic headline: "Toll of the Ober Law—No Communists, Two Quakers."

Many non-Quakers support the work of the American Friends Service Committee and its multiplicity of activities— refugee relief, self-help housing, criminal justice, integrated high-quality education, programs for ethnic minorities, campaigns against poverty and hunger and discrimination.

When the service agencies of the Society of Friends were awarded the Nobel Peace Prize in 1947, the chairman of the selection committee said, "Even if the statesmen succeed in constructing a better international order, it will not have a firm foundation if man has not imbibed the true spirit of fellowship. How to achieve that is the great question.

"We know that it can be done. We have seen that a small group of people has demonstrated in a practical way the spirit which does away with the occasion of war and shown that unselfishness and goodness exist and that there are people who do not discriminate between races, between fellow countrymen and foreigners, between enemies and friends" (Kavanaugh, p. 18).

◥ **THE PRISONERS' DILEMMA—A DISCUSSION OF OPTIONS**
If you decide you would take the medicine for yourself that would indicate a Stage One attitude, even if you justified the decision by reasoning that you are probably the strongest and would have the best chance to survive to let the world know about conditions in the camp.

If you feel it best to share the medicine equally because this is what any fair and decent person would do, taking your chances on survival, that would be a Stage Three approach.

If you believe you should draw lots, with the winner using the supply of medicine for himself, as the orderly and sensible way to handle it, that would lean toward Stage Four thinking. If you decide to draw lots as the best means of safeguarding each individual's rights for a chance at survival, that would be reasoning at Stages Five and Six.

)ther Voices,
Other Concepts

Fran and Jeff Edwards have been watching a television talk show. He snaps off the set and pours a glass of wine for each of them.

F: What makes those women's lib types so full of hostility? And why do so many of them work so hard to see how unattractive they can be?

N: That's not fair. You think a woman's whole job is to look pretty for the fellows.

F: Well, why not? We're always trying to look good for you.

N: I guess the real problem is that women are supposed to be little helpers, staying in the background, not concerned about themselves. If they do try to think about their own needs, they're considered selfish, unfeminine, aggressive.

F: Seems to me you get pretty much what you want.

N: I don't know how to explain it. I guess it's being afraid to speak up and say what you *really* want or feeling if you even seriously consider your own needs you're not being a real woman. If a man goes after what he wants, he's considered dynamic, successful—but if a woman does she's unfeeling and aggressive.

F: So what's the answer?

N: I think women need to work at being fair to themselves and be completely honest about it, and men need to work at being more caring and let their emotional side show a little.

JEFF: Unisex?

FRAN: Not really *unisex*. Just using both kinds of thinking.

Is there a difference in men and women's moral reasoning? Carol Gilligan (1977), of the Harvard Center for Moral Education, suggests some answers. Writing in the *Harvard Educational Review*, she gives a carefully reasoned presentation of her thesis that the unavoidable male-oriented viewpoint of Kohlberg's research and the use of exclusively male subjects in his original longitudinal study has led to a neglect of important factors in the feminine perspective of morality. Most women are characteristically classified at Stage Three—studies indicate they get there earlier and remain there longer, while males go on to theoretically higher, more abstract stages. Gilligan claims that this asserted failure of women to develop as "high" on the moral development scale as males doesn't necessarily demonstrate reasoning that is inferior, only a viewpoint that is different. With the emphasis on nurturing and caring so traditional in the woman's role, they see personal relationships as vitally important; to many of them morality is avoiding hurting others. A Radcliffe undergraduate in a 1970 Gilligan study said, "When I think of the word *morality*, I think of obligations. I usually think of it as conflicts between personal desires and social things . . . personal desires . . . versus personal desires of another. Morality is that whole realm of how you decide these conflicts" (Gilligan, p. 485).

Another Radcliffe student explained her view of what constitutes morality: "I personally don't want to hurt other people. This is a main criterion for me. . . . It underlies my sense of justice. It isn't nice to inflict pain. I empathize with anyone in pain" (Gilligan, p. 485).

Gilligan has described women's moral stage development in a manner similar to the models of Dewey, Piaget, Kohlberg—the traditional phase concept with individuals moving from egocentric levels to society-oriented stages to a universal ethical viewpoint. In Gilligan's sequence, women's moral judgment proceeds from a focus on the self, at the first level, to the discovery, in the transition to the second level, of the idea of responsibility as the basis for a new relationship with others. In moving to the third stage, the real crisis comes. This is the development of independence, of giving importance to one's own needs. This step is difficult because the ideal of feminine virtue has always been that it's only to others we are obligated to give moral care. But, when women perceive this as unjust, they go through another transition to arrive at a universal condemnation of exploitation and hurt for themselves as well as for others. In this way, they move from selfishness to responsibility and then from "goodness" to truth and justice.

In a study of 29 women of diverse age, race, and social class, referred by abortion and pregnancy counseling services, Gilligan sought to learn how each one dealt with the problems she faced and, through her research, to learn more about the nature and development of women's moral judgment.

An 18-year-old, asked what she thought when she found herself pregnant, said, "I really didn't think anything except that I didn't want it. . . . I wasn't ready for it, and next year will be my last year and I want to go to school" (Gilligan, p. 492).

A more mature outlook than that egocentric attitude was demonstrated by another young girl who originally wanted to have her baby as a way of combating loneliness. She came to see that her motives were selfish and unrealistic, that it would not be a good idea for her to try to keep the child. "Sometimes what is necessary comes before what you want, because it might not always lead to the right thing. . . . I have never really had too many hard decisions in my life. . . . It has taken some responsibility to do this" (Gilligan, p. 494).

A woman who had decided on an abortion because having a second child at that time was against her doctor's advice and would strain the emotional and financial resources of the family dealt with the problem of the conflict between that decision and her feeling about an abortion as the taking of a human life: "Even though it is not formed, it is the potential . . . but I have to think of (my life), of my son's and my husband's. At first I thought it was for selfish reasons, but it is not" (Gilligan, p. 499). This woman was trying to consider her own needs as well as those of the others in the situation, to be responsible to those others and therefore be "good," but also to be responsible to herself and thus be "honest" and "real."

From the woman's perspective, Kohlberg's dilemmas, hypothetical and abstract, separate the participants from the reality of their daily lives, separate moral problems from social reality. The feminine response is to want to know the dilemma in its full context, to flesh out the human side of a problem in a way that involves compassion and tolerance and concern about social injustice. Because of the concept of responsibility and care in the woman's perspective, Gilligan argues the need for an expanded developmental theory that would include the feminine voice—it's important for both sexes to have an adult moral concept involving caring and compassion as well as autonomy, dealing with the complexities of real life as well as abstract concepts of right and wrong.

While this book relies heavily on Kohlberg's model of stage development, we have also considered the work of many others in the field. For example, Peck and Havighurst did a longitudinal study in the 1950s, described in *The Psychology of Character Development* (1970). While their terminology deals with "character" rather than "stage," the character can change as the individual develops psychologically and morally. In the Peck and Havighurst sequence, there is the *amoral* character, typical of babies or young children following their own whims and impulses; the *expedient* type, primarily self-centered individuals considering other people's welfare and reactions only in order to gain their own personal ends; the *conforming* type, who wants to do what everyone else is doing, what a person "should" do; the *irrational conscientious* character blindly following internalized rules, forgetting these rules are made by humans, for their own benefit, and can be changed. The highest level is exemplified by the *rational-altruistic* type, those who not only have a stable set of moral principles but are concerned as to whether an act serves others as well as themselves. These five character types are close kin of Kohlberg's main categories of development (blending five and six together.)

There are many others, too numerous to describe their individual contributions. Best known are probably the classic stages of Sigmund Freud, Erikson's eight stages, the work of Fromm and Reisman—all of them seeing individuals as moving through the same life journey, some remaining fixed at lower levels of development, but all passing through the same way stations, responding to the challenges of life and finding better and more adequate responses as they move to higher stages of moral judgment.

Kohlberg's theories, while much admired and studied, have found critics among some educators, philosophers, and psychologists. For example, in spite of the fact that his research was replicated in a variety of cultures, there is disagreement as to whether his sample was sufficiently large to justify his sweeping conclusion that the same concept of justice he finds to be the highest level of reasoning, Stages Five and Six, is present in all the cultures of the world.

Jack Fraenkel, writing in *Social Education*, 1976, has reservations about Kohlberg's claim that moral development is always upward, from lower stages to higher. Fraenkel cites the example of the Ik tribe, as described by Colin Turnbull in his book *The Mountain People.* When the Ik, a tribe of peaceful hunters, were moved from their ancestral lands to a crowded and difficult terrain where it was hard to obtain enough food, their culture broke down, showing how quickly loving relationships and concern for others can give way to hostile, egocentric, self-serving behavior. As a two-year drought destroyed the Ik's scanty crops and starvation set in, hoarding food and keeping it from one's family became honorable. Old people were abandoned to die, and burial ceremonies to honor the dead were no longer held. Turnbull says, "The Ik teach us that our much vaunted human values are not inherent in humanity at all but are associated with a particular form of survival called *society* and that all, even society itself, are luxuries that can be dispensed with."*

Other criticisms of Kohlberg's theories are based on the seemingly low correlation between moral judgment and actual behavior. Kohlberg says people usually reason, and might be presumed to act, on the highest level of moral reasoning they are capable of understanding. Dissenters argue that a great many people capable of Stage Five reasoning often display behavior more typical of Stage Two. Kohlberg doesn't deny that under the pressure of extreme circumstances regression can take place from one level of development to another, and, as mentioned in Chapter Two, businesspeople and other individuals capable of a high level of moral reasoning may make decisions typical of a lower level because of the "moral atmosphere" in which they find themselves.

The advocates of the stage development theory don't claim that they have the answers to all questions about moral reasoning. Some of the criticism is undoubtedly justified, but it doesn't destroy the edifice of well-researched theory that has been created. Moral stage development remains a valid hypothesis whose practical value is being tested in many ways. More research is still needed, and much is under way, but there is nothing comparable that offers so much promise in the field of moral education.

---

*Colin Turnbull, *The Mountain People*. New York; Simon and Schuster, 1972.

Applications

Now that you have an understanding of the stages of moral development, how can you use it? What are some of its practical applications? It's adaptable to almost any setting: at home, in sexual relationships, in schools, at church, in prisons, at the grocery store. Here are some of the ways it's currently being applied.

As you now know, moral development occurs within us as individuals and in our personal moral understanding. It's not indoctrination we need, but stimulation: discussion and debate that take place in the kind of democratic structure that gives each of us the chance to grow and uncovers the ways in which we deceive ourselves and each other. We all play moral games some of the time and justify the things we do with rationalizations ranging from the lofty to the ignominious and the cynical—in the name of God, for our country, for national security, for our family, or just for ourselves: "Everybody's doing it." "They told me to do it." "My childhood was deprived, and now I must be compensated."

One of the places where the principles of stage development are being applied and tested is in education—an area critically in need of moral reasoning that can be translated into responsible behavior. "Only psychology and ethics can take education out of the rule-of-thumb stage and elevate the school to a vital, effective institution in the greatest of all constructions—the building of a free and powerful character," wrote Dewey, over 50 years ago (1895, pp. 207–208). How have things progressed since then?

Along with declining test scores there is almost an epidemic of anarchy and destruction in our schools. We're all too familiar with accounts of vandalism and violence in spite of increasing expenditures for security. Can the moral development theory be applied to reduce such outbreaks and help children learn to take personal responsibility, to see the schools as theirs?

In an effort to achieve Dewey's goal of making schools a place where real character development takes place, an increasing number of educational districts are adopting programs based on or incorporating Kohlberg's stage development theories and teaching methods. For a generation or two, moral education was carefully avoided, disavowed both by educators and the public. People viewed it as indoctrination, a forced feeding of particular ideologies and a violation of the venerable tradition of separation of church and state, even though moral education is not dependent on religion or religious principles. Whether intentional or not, our children all receive moral indoctrination in school, even if it's only exposure to the value systems of the teachers. Advocates of the stage development approach claim that with their method there is no attempt to implant a value system. What happens is that the pupils are exposed to moral dilemmas and to viewpoints other than their own, thereby stimulating growth and understanding.

The work of Moshe Blatt was described in Chapter Three, in relation to the classroom debate about the man whose son was severely injured and who commandeered a stranger's car to take the boy to a hospital. Such techniques, based on Kohlberg's theories and using Socratic dialogue, have proved to be effective methods for raising students' levels of moral reasoning.

Kohlberg and his associates decided that if brief periods of classroom discussion could have such an effect, a more pervasive, enduring and psychologically sound concern for the entire school's influence on moral growth should have even deeper and more positive effects, involving the social atmosphere and the "justice" structure of the school.

There has been much discussion of the "hidden curriculum" in the educational system—including the manner in which schools are administered. Most are still run on authoritarian lines, with students having little chance to contribute their ideas about how the school program is administered. They learn that they'd better obey a strict set of rules or be punished; to get along, they must conform outwardly to the opinion of the majority whether or not they share it. While they are taught the importance of democracy and freedom of speech, the rights of minorities and the right to hold unpopular or unconventional opinions, the actual learning process directs their moral development in a different pattern. The school has a moral atmosphere that combines the punishment morality of Stage One with the law-and-order morality of Stage Four.

To let students take part in running their own school in a "Just Community" atmosphere, the Cluster School was started in Cambridge, Massachusetts, in 1974. A group of students, parents, and teachers, under the guidance of Kohlberg and his Harvard associates, started the school as a separate unit of the Cambridge High and Latin School. They created a school government run on a democratic basis—one person, one vote, for both students and teachers, and focused on moral issues in history and literature classes. There are also courses in peer counseling, democracy, journalism, writing, and health education. Although students join in the parent school's athletic and extracurricular activities, the group was deliberately kept small enough so there would be a real feeling of participation. Even smaller groups of 10 or 12 meet to prepare ideas and suggestions for the Cluster School community meetings.

Students and teachers discuss important problems—drugs, stealing, violations of group-adopted rules. They approach problems in terms of fairness to the individuals involved as well as to the community. There are the free-wheeling moral debates, with everyone arguing at different levels of the moral development scale. Students make and enforce their own rules, with the staff trying to promote concern for the fairness of the rules and encourage a sense of responsibility.

How does it work? In the beginning, it was close to anarchy. It took two months before there was an agreement to discipline students for using or selling drugs. But when the majority finally made such rules, the students followed them. Gradually the students took more responsibility for their own behavior and learned to join in at community discussions and to do a good job of presiding over meetings and keeping order. Students from different backgrounds formed firm friendships; some problem personalities began to show signs of positive change. The students themselves say their behavior improved because the Cluster School treated them with fairness and gave them a chance to protest when they thought they were being treated unjustly.

There are naturally reservations about such a drastic approach: "It's difficult in creating a utopian school to have to work with nonutopian kids," according to Jack Parham, principal of an experimental school for problem students in Irvine, California. "There are Stage One and Stage Two kids who understand somebody throwing them up against a wall, but they can't relate to community norms" (*Newsweek*, 1976, p. 75). But the experiment has worked well enough to encourage continued efforts to test, expand, and improve the concept. Kohlberg doesn't claim that the Cluster School is a Utopia as yet, and says there are many ways to improve it. However, it's still a much better option than the others available.

Kohlberg was asked whether he would like to see moral discussion groups in all of the public schools and he replied: "Yes, I think so, as long as the teachers have at least a minimal ability to listen and to ask questions, and don't try to indoctrinate." This is further evidence of his commendable reluctance to force ideas on anyone, child or adult, and of his belief that the way to help anyone grow is through stimulating discussion where everyone is free to differ and conclusions are arrived at only after a full exchange of views.

The moral stage development methods also offer a new approach to the problems of our prison system, which critics say neither reforms nor rehabilitates. In 1970, a team from the Connecticut Department of Corrections, the Russell Sage Foundation, and Harvard University, began to apply the stage theory to the rehabilitation of prisoners, initiating the program by starting moral discussion groups at the Cheshire Reformatory for Men. Follow-up studies showed that the same prisoners who had moved upward in their moral reasoning were those who were having less trouble with the law (Kohlberg et al., "The Just Community Approach to Corrections").

In 1971, the Harvard team decided to try a more comprehensive plan, to see what full-time exposure to a moral development program could accomplish for prisoners. A special cottage was set up at the Connecticut Women's Correction Center at Niantic with inmates chosen for the program from a group of volunteers, staffed by personnel especially trained for the experiment.

After the first two years, the experiment could be considered a success. Only 16 percent of the women involved had returned to prison or become involved with criminal offenses. Applying that same moral development approach to the problem of the transition from prison to normal community life, an offshoot of the Niantic Cottage was created—a half-way house where women from the Correction Center unit could live while serving the final portion of their sentences.

To bring about a genuine feeling of community the researchers found it necessary to set up a self-contained unit separate from the rest of the institution. Inmates take part in the decision-making process and the situation is designed so that they not only have a say in running things but are helped to see their responsibility to the other members of the group.

As the Connecticut prisoners began to understand and accept the moral nature of their miniature "just community," they could better understand the morality of the larger—and not always so just—society in which they would soon be living and approach it with a different attitude. In lively moral debates the women were exposed to new and different points of view. They lived in an atmosphere of fairness where there was both loyalty and trust; took the responsibility for making and enforcing their own rules. When researchers talked with former inmates two years after their release many of them said it was the first time they had ever lived in an environment where people treated each other with fairness and mutual concern. Because they wanted to go on living that way and having such relationships, they tried to choose a life for themselves that would make it possible.

For any rehabilitation to be real and lasting there has to be a basic change in thinking. With the guidance of the Harvard-trained staff, prisoners at Niantic work out moral and practical problems of day-to-day life; following the Blatt-Kohlberg model, they are exposed to higher levels of moral judgment. Gradually they learn to understand their own reasoning and how it has affected their lives. No amount of preaching will produce a change in our moral attitude unless there is a change in our thinking, and this each one of us must do for him- or herself. Challenge, stimulation, and constant exposure to higher stages are the tools used in the Niantic experiment.

A typical staff-inmate dilemma is that of Carol Owens and Ina Martin. Like most correctional officers, Carol Owens is actively involved with the problems of the women assigned to her and had developed a close relationship with Ina Martin. On the basis of Owens' recommendation, inmate Martin was approved for a Christmas furlough. When she returned after the holiday, Martin confided to Owens that she had violated the rules of her furlough by going to another state. Reasoning at Stage Three and regarding family ties as more important than furlough rules, Martin had gone to visit her two younger children and her ailing mother in Boston, after visiting her two older children in Hartford.

Owens, the staff member, had to decide whether she should report the violation when Martin had trusted her and confessed to her, counting on Owens to maintain her trust. On the other hand, reasoning at Stage Four, Owens had an obligation to her job, to the rules of the state and of the prison. Owens did report Martin, who became bitter and angry. The problem could have been much better resolved in a group, by helping the two women to understand each other's thinking— letting Martin see her obligation to the community and to the state as well as to those relatives she felt she had to visit; helping Owens to understand Martin's reasons for breaking the rule or to move to a Stage Five perspective and realize that inmates have rights even when they break the rules.

Inmates helping clarify the choice another inmate must make, offering advice and support, are shown in a transcript of a small discussion group at Niantic (Kohlberg et al., "The Just Community Approach to Corrections," pp. 95–97). A pregnant white inmate arrives in the middle, upset after a visit from her parents. The father of the child is black. The parents demand she have the child and then give it up for adoption. One issue is whether she is to make the choice or the parents are. Another issue is, even if she wants the baby, whether she really can handle the long-time responsibility of being a mother.

NMATE S: Priscilla, what's the matter?

NMATE M: Your folks come?

NMATE G: What happened?

NMATE S: Wait a minute before you start answering and going through the third degree. Do you want to cry first?

NMATE P: (Inaudible)

NMATE G: What happened on your visit, huh?

NMATE S: They don't want the baby? They want you to have an abortion or what? Give him away?

NMATE P: Give him up.

INMATE G: So what do you think about that?

INMATE P: I don't know because (my father) had a lot of things to say about . . .

INMATE G: I can imagine what he had to say.

INMATE P: I guess I just always respected him . . .

INMATE G: All that is due to the fact that the baby is supposed to be mixed, right?

INMATE P: Mostly.

INMATE G: Did you know that your parents were prejudiced before you started messing around with a black guy?

INMATE P: Yeah.

INMATE G: That didn't make any difference?

INMATE P: What?

INMATE G: That didn't make any difference?

INMATE P: To me?

INMATE G: Yeah. And you never thought that at any time when you were going with him what the outcome might be if you did get pregnant, what your situation would be? You never even thought about that, huh?

INMATE P: I knew all that. . . . It's just that I didn't . . . I cared in a way but not . . . but I didn't feel reticent.

INMATE S: Well, Priscilla, the only thing I can say is that if you plan on going on your own, and having responsibility to yourself, and not depending on your family for anything, I would say have the baby and truck it along. But if you are going to have to get some kind of help or going to your family, I think the best thing you could do under the circumstances is do as they say. But, if you are responsible enough to go out there and make it on your own, keep the child. . . . Because, I mean it seems hard, but you're 19, and you are old enough to be on the state, and the state can't take your child away unless you sign it away. And when you get out there, they will give you your child. The state won't be spending more extra money than they have to. So when you get your child, keep your child if you are ready for the responsibility of taking care of a child and yourself. But if you are going to have the baby just so you can say you got it, no.

INMATE P: I know that, but see, he said that he doesn't ... he thinks having the baby and keeping it is going to ... that I won't be able to do it, and as far as school and getting through high school and like getting a job, he said it is all going to go down the drain if I keep the baby.

INMATE S: Anyway, he's about right because when you have a baby the party time is over. There is no more party times. The party time is over if you're going to be a proper mother. But like I say, anybody can have a child, but everybody can't be a mother.

INMATE M: Yeah, but her education won't go down the drain. She can always use that. . . .

INMATE S: With that child! As far as education, she will never have to work for 18 more years.

INMATE G: I don't think that's clarifying . . .

INMATE S: Yeah, but wait a minute. Here is what I am trying to say. The state will back you up. Now if you have a child and you want to go to school, you can go to school. The state will pay for somebody to babysit. This is what they want.

INMATE G: I am not speaking about her and the state not taking care of her. What I am saying is I don't think that that's what her father means as far as it is "all going to go down the drain." The only thing that I can see her father objecting about is that her baby is going to be mixed. That's what they are saying to her, that she is not going to make it because of that. That is going to be a hindrance to her whether she has her education or not. They don't want no part of it, so they can't see why anybody else would want any part of it.

INMATE S: This is what I am saying, if she's got it in her mind that she wants this child. . . . In other words, fuck what my family says, I want this baby and I am going to take care of this baby. She can go on ahead and do it and don't need her family to do nothing for her.

Most of this advice is at Stage Two, suggesting that Priscilla ignore her parents' opinion unless she has to be dependent on them. Life-long state aid is also accepted without question. But there is a real sense of the responsibility necessary to be a mother and an emphasis that the inmate has to accept that responsibility when she makes her choice. This is an example of how spontaneous counseling and crisis intervention occur in a moral development setting.

A rehabilitation program based on similar concepts, dealing with mentally disturbed individuals who have been referred by the courts because of actual or potentially violent behavior, is that of the Utah State Hospital in Provo, Utah. Patients help set their own rules and maintain security—part of a program that tries to discourage antisocial behavior by giving the participants full responsibility for their own conduct.

According to program director Dr. John Woods (*Newsweek,* 1977, p. 78), group accountability is the key. When there is trouble, a patient-directed "posse" is called into action. If a violent patient strikes another, the posse is alerted—members guard the exit doors while others go to help patients who might get upset. The rest calm the offender without any help from the staff. The program has been strikingly successful: Of those who have had at least six months experience, the recidivism rate has been only 15 percent, compared to a national average of 75 percent. One inmate said, "This place forces you to make the right decisions, so that after a while you begin to make them automatically." Even though patients are permitted a lot of freedom, in ten years only six have tried to escape, and all of those were returned.

What about applications at home? How can parents help children progress to higher stages of moral comprehension? It helps just to try to see how your children are thinking and realize that obeying rules isn't the same thing as moral development. Ths most effective way to handle problems is to appeal to the next higher stage in your child's development. A young boy who hates to cut the lawn can be helped up a stage by giving him a stronger motive than simple obedience—a financial Stage Two reward to do his chores, making his allowance depend on it. And, as he grows older, he can be rewarded by praising the way he does things just as efficiently as his father—a Stage Three motivation. Telling him warmly that you couldn't get along without him and his help is Stage Four—making him an important part of the whole picture, someone who can be relied on and trusted to do his part.

Even trips in the car can provide opportunities. For example, children can observe for themselves that you are a reasonable driver, and you can make it clear you're stopping for stop signs and watching the speed limit not because you'll get caught and fined (Stage One) but because if we didn't obey traffic rules we'd have chaos on the highways—Stage Four concern for an orderly society.

Even television can be an effective tool. Instead of sitting back passively, you can join in and encourage the children to make a game out of analyzing what they're watching. If you don't have children, you and your friends can play with the moral dilemmas on the tube—there's a wide variety, from police shows to the problems of Richard III. You might even find yourself talking back to the set as you try to decide what stage reasoning is involved, why you think what the Fonz is doing is a good and useful way to behave or why it isn't.

In an episode on the popular *Laverne and Shirley* series, the girls were anxious to win a dance contest because a television set was offered as the prize. To persuade two somewhat unenthusiastic young men, excellent dancers, to be their partners in the competition, Laverne and Shirley hinted strongly there would be some amorous adventures at the end of the evening.

The deal was made and the television set was won, but when the two couples returned to the apartment the girls didn't want to follow through on the implied bargain. To cool off their eager escorts, Laverne and Shirley came on with an aggressive, exaggerated sexual approach, alarming the boys so much that they fled. After they had left, Laverne commented, "I guess that wasn't very nice, what we did." "Maybe not," Shirley replied, "but look what we got!"—indicating the television set.

Charles Osgood reported a story on CBS *Profile* that would make a good starting point for a moral debate, one with more area for disagreement than the *Laverne and Shirley* episode:

"Claude Samuel Donatelli is 41 years old. He never went to college. You can find him these days pumping gas at a service station in San Diego.

"But Donatelli is not your average, ordinary, run-of-the-mill gas station attendant. Last year he decided to get a job as a nuclear physicist. He applied at a company in Del Mar, California, called Environmental Control Management. Naturally, they asked him about his educational background, and, since he figured they wouldn't hire somebody for that sort of work who hadn't been to college, Donatelli told them he was a Ph.D. from the University of California at Berkeley. Well, the company liked the way he looked and talked, and so they hired him, and introduced him in the lab as Doctor Donatelli.

"Now, if you or I tried to get away with this, the whole jig would probably have been up the first time we got into a conversation with one of our fellow nuclear physicists on the subject of nuclear physics. It's not the sort of thing you can fake very easily.

"But not only did Donatelli pass muster with his coworkers, he knocked them out with his brilliance. Within four months of the time he donned his white coat, the company was so impressed with his theory on the neutralizing of atomic warheads they made him a vice-president of the firm and started considering his theory for possible submission to the government.

"They're still thinking about that, even though Donatelli himself has been found out. Some federal investigator, checking up on his application, discovered that Claude Samuel Donatelli did not get a Ph.D. from Berkeley—or from any place else, for that matter—and had never even graduated from anything higher than high school. Donatelli was charged with felonious violation of the California Education Code, pleaded guilty, and . . . the judge deferred sentence for a month to give the defendant a chance to think about how he could best contribute to society, working eight hours a week for some religious or charitable organization, or something. The judge will implement Donatelli's idea—if he likes it—as a condition of probation.

"Offhand, coming up with a way of neutralizing atomic warheads doesn't sound like a bad contribution to society, for openers. But then we can't have pump-jockeys without degrees running around thinking about stuff like that, can we?"

How do you feel about it? Do you think Donatelli's contribution justified lying about his qualifications in order to get the job? Is it more important to have the right credentials or to have creative ideas? Should the company have kept Donatelli on as a consultant, degree or no degree?

Radio broadcast, television program, family disagreement, a story in the newspaper—anything can be used to trigger a lively discussion in which you defend your point of view as well as trying to understand others. Moral issues come into sharper focus. Why did you do that? For a reward? Because everyone's doing it? Because you might want a favor in return some day? Because it would be best for everyone involved? Because someone's human dignity is threatened?

And, as we consider, we grow a little along the way. One of the major applications of the moral stage development theory is becoming aware of our own thinking. And one of the most significant effects of moving to higher levels of moral reasoning is the broader perspective it provides.

Imagine a city, multiterraced. At the lowest level—let's call it the Terrace of the Lower Hill—we can see only what physically affects each of us. The view is restricted, shut off by winding streets and vertical cliffs.

The next level, the Terrace of the Marketplace, is an area

zoned for commerce. People are bargaining with each other, working out mutually beneficial deals. We can begin to see a little of each other's needs. The view is much better than that from the Terrace of the Lower Hill, but it is still limited, portions blackened by tall smokestacks and rows of billboards.

Walking up a broad flight of steps we come to the third level, the Terrace of Friendship—an enclave of patterns and passwords. There's a lot of embracing, people apparently delighted with each other. Why not just stay here? But we can't see far enough—the view is limited, only reaching the edge of our own residential and business districts, and a little beyond.

We climb more steps to the Terrace of the Stone Tablets on the fourth level, where broad boulevards stretch before us with dignified public buildings of grey stone on either side. Flags are flying everywhere. They are beautiful, streaming in the wind. The view is much extended but it is still restricted by all the buildings. We can't yet see beyond our own geographical boundaries.

The climb up to the fifth level, the Terrace of Contracts, is a steep one. We arrive out of breath and find ourselves facing a majestic courthouse of white marble fronted with massive pillars. In the distance are rivers and forests; above us, a free and endless expanse of sky. Even though the view is very wide, we still can't see quite as far as we would like.

The path is almost vertical as we struggle up to the Terrace of Justice, a long, narrow butte lying between lofty peaks. The air is cold and clear, and we can see for hundreds of miles in every direction. Up here the circle of our vision has widened until it encompasses the globe, includes the whole human race, all the creatures of the earth. No one is outside the boundaries of our concern.

This is one way to visualize levels of moral development: whatever else is accomplished, moving to higher stages of moral reasoning continually expands your viewpoint. You are able not only to understand the viewpoint of others but, as your own vision widens, their welfare comes to seem as important as your own.

There is still much to be learned about the psychology of moral stage development and how it functions, but with the tools it has already provided us we can do many things. We can take some steps to improve our educational system. And each of us can be aware of where we are standing when we make moral decisions. We can learn to find better and more adequate bases for answering the serious questions that confront us throughout our lives and thus widen our circle of concern.

Dilemmas

for a Moral Workout

All of us constantly face moral problems that demand resolution; the action we take depends on our reasoning process. Here are some additional dilemmas for you to play with, all based on real incidents. As you read them, think what choice you yourself would make, and why. When you've had a chance to consider each one and to choose the solution that seems closest to your own thinking, read the estimate of what stage is indicated for that particular response. Very few are Stage One, and none are Stage Six—most are typical of the levels most commonly used—Stages Two, Three, Four, or Five.

Try them on your friends—not only to see if you can bring them around to your own sensible point of view, but to discuss what solution would be the most satisfactory from the standpoint of each of the characters involved. Look at each situation from every perspective, even though most of them focus on the point of view of the person with the tough choice to make. Obviously, there are no "right" answers to any of them.

Try creating your own dilemmas; or, even better, consider the moral problems you or your friends or your family have actually faced and analyze the decisions you made. Can you relate those decisions to a moral stage or to a similar kind of judgment? Consider other levels of reasoning that might have brought a different solution. Sometimes two people reasoning at the same moral stage come up with completely different answers to a problem. And sometimes individuals at different stages reach the same decision but by different routes.

The object of all this is not judgment, but understanding. Philosophy itself stems from our ability to wonder about ourselves, our interaction with others, about the strange, marvelous, surprising, or appalling things we all do. With the ability to take a really good look at the moral reasoning involved in all kinds of situations, you can add a new dimension to the continuing debates that are not unique to campus bull sessions but go on all the time in business, in bed, at dinner parties, in pubs.

The Affair

Suppose you are Bruce, a writer who has been married for 15 years and has three teenaged children. You and your wife, Cassie, have had a good, sturdy relationship for the most part. You've lived all over the world and have a host of shared experiences, memories, and friends. Because you work at home, you're close to your children and spend almost as much time with them as Cassie does. Sharon, your insecure 13-year-old daughter, is going through a stage where she and her mother are fierce antagonists, and she clings to you for affection and security and praise. You can almost see her blossom when you tell her how beautiful she is, braces and all. Your two boys are sports fanatics and share baseball statistics, tennis rankings, and football lore with you every morning over the breakfast table. You take them to games whenever you can, play ball with them, teach them golf and tennis.

In your occasional travels without your family, there have been some extramarital romps but nothing that has really threatened your marriage. The last time you lived abroad, in India, Cassie had polio. Although she made a good recovery she has a moderately crippled leg. You have a hang-up about physical perfection; you try to be sympathetic and patient but you find her much less sexually appealing these days.

Now you're really torn. You've been having an affair for several months with Jean, a young divorcee in a nearby town who does research for you. You feel almost pulled apart, guilty, uneasy; unable to face the thought of giving up Jean, unable to consider leaving your family. Cassie, with her honesty, her patient fidelity, her limp, has an almost Dickensian appeal, fills you with pity and a need to take care of her.

One night when you're having dinner with Jean, she tells you the whole situation has been frustrating and humiliating for her—she hates being the cliché "other woman." Either you divorce Cassie, or Jean will put an end to your affair. Reluctantly you tell her you can't bring yourself to hurt your wife and damage your relationship with your children. You'll have to stop seeing Jean.

This resolve lasts for a month or so; you hear rumors Jean has been out with a doctor you know slightly. Finally, desperate, you call and say you have to talk to her. When you arrive at her house, she tells you she is indeed going with another man—what did you expect?—and is considering marriage. You have a passionate reconciliation and renew all your pledges of love for each other. Jean finally says if you'll get a divorce she'll break off completely with the doctor.

OPTIONAL ENDINGS

A. You decide to stay with your family. You really want to be a good husband and father, not force Cassie into a life of loneliness and hurt, put no more trauma into Debbie's difficult adolescence. Your relationship with Jean is exciting, and it hurts to give it up, but it's more important to do what you see as the right thing.

B. The world won't come to an end if you leave Cassie. You can still support your family, visit your children, be almost as much of a father as you were before. Jean is what you really want and need at this point in your life, and you decide to get a divorce.

C. You decide to keep your family together. You think it over
and decide it's wrong to break up a family except for the most
extreme reasons. You don't want to contribute to the social
chaos you see all around you. Your feeling for Jean is strong
but what you do with your life and how you fulfill your obligations are more important—how you behave to people who
trust you.

D. You find it painful to give up Jean, but you see your marriage
as an important and long-standing contract and your love and
concern for all the members of the family are the most important factors. More people would be hurt if you left. You will
stay with them.

ASSESSMENT OF OPTIONS A. This response is indicative of trying
to live up to social group expectations, typical of Stage Three. B.
This is a pragmatic, self-centered view of the situation indicating a
Stage Two approach. C. This viewpoint is concerned with the
family as a unit of society and with maintaining the status quo, a
Stage Four type of reasoning. D. This indicates a kind of social
contract thinking, trying to consider the rights and the welfare of everyone in the situation, found at Stage Five.

The Dudleys and the Marlowes

In this dilemma, you can choose which family member's solution you prefer.

Two families recently moved into Lake Forest, a housing tract—the Dudleys and the Marlowes. The children from both families get on wonderfully, play together, enjoy outings.

Mr. Marlowe learns that Mr. Dudley is an officer in Executives' Exchange, an influential businessmen's club. To help his own social and business standing in the community, Marlow wants to cultivate this neighbor. Mrs. Marlowe notices the youngest Dudley (Paul, four) has been unable to play well with the other children. She learns that he is left-handed and his parents believe it should be corrected by any means possible—putting his left arm in a sling, for example. When their oldest daughter, Cindy, is home on vacation from her graduate studies in psychology, Mrs. Marlowe mentions the matter. Cindy has the Definitive Word—all scientific evidence indicates it's bad to try to break a child of left-handedness. The cure is worse than the so-called problem. The three of them agree that the Dudleys are handling it all wrong, but they disagree on what to do about it.

OPTIONAL SOLUTIONS:

A. Mrs. Marlowe thinks the information her daughter has should be brought to the Dudley's attention, but Mrs. Marlowe herself doesn't want to do it. She says it would be interfering with their parental authority and their right to do as they please with their own children. She knows she would be embarrassed and resentful if someone interfered in *her* family affairs in that way.

B. Mr. Marlowe says mentioning the psychological studies to the Dudleys would alienate them and spoil their friendship. Since he needs Dudley, he is not going to do anything to interfere with Dudley's child-rearing methods, right or wrong.

C. Cindy Marlowe thinks the Dudleys should be told, whether they want to be interfered with or not. She respects their sovereignty as parents, she says, but believes that Paul has fundamental rights to healthy and normal development that are being interfered with by his parents. She resolves to give them the information, and she wants help in figuring out a relatively polite way to do it.

ASSESSMENT OF OPTIONS A. Stage Two: The family has the right to do as they please with what is "theirs." B. Stage Two: expedient, concern with not antagonizing someone who can be helpful to you. C. Stage Five: concern for individual rights; a decision to act according to principles of fairness.

The Union Dilemma

You are a friend of the Conlons. Mr. and Mrs. Conlon have had a produce stand in Pottsville for nearly half a century, and the local residents agree that, for fresh, high-quality fruits and vegetables, the Conlons are the best. They have survived through the years, despite the supermarkets in Pottsville's shopping center, because of the care they take in choosing from the produce the local farmers have to offer. If the corn doesn't look tender enough or the tomatoes have bruises, the Conlons turn them down. A lot of people in the area appreciate that kind of quality, and the Conlons have a loyal clientele. They are your good friends and neighbors, since you live just down the street and you always buy from them. They pick out a special melon or a box of berries just for you because you've been friends for so long.

Some farm labor representatives come through Pottsville and post notices urging everyone to boycott nonunion produce. The newspapers pick up the story and print stories about the intolerable living conditions of the migrants who work the fields; tin shacks with three or four families crowded together, no toilets, and only cold water for bathing; children as young as five working on the rows with their parents.

Many Pottsville citizens are shocked at these reports and agree to support a boycott to bring pressure on the growers to accept the workers' right to form a union. One group calls on the Conlons to enlist their support and urges them to sell only union-picked fruits and vegetables. Although the Conlons are sympathetic to the cause, they explain that all the growers for miles around are nonunion. There's no way for them to purchase fresh, vine, or tree-ripened vegetables and fruits that are union grown.

The manager of a supermarket decides that, since refrigerated trucks bring produce to his store from many areas, he has access to union-grown crops from other regions. After getting approval from the chain's general manager, he posts a big sign in his window: "SUPPORT THE BOYCOTT—WE HAVE UNION PRODUCE."

The town of Pottsville is divided: If they support the boycott, the Conlons will suffer financially and might have to shut down after serving the community for 40 years; if their customers remain loyal, such action will help to keep the farm workers exploited. There is a lot of argument on both sides. These are your friends—what should you do?

TIONAL ENDINGS

The Conlons are your good friends. They're getting old, and you would hate to see them in financial difficulties because of this problem, which is really not their fault. You can't let them down—you're going to go on buying your fruits and vegetables from them to let them know you're behind them.

The Conlons have always sold you good merchandise, and you intend to go on trading there. It's too bad about the farm workers, but the few tomatoes or peaches you buy in a week isn't going to make that much difference in their lives.

You try to balance the hardships and injustice suffered by the workers against the hardship for the Conlons. There are a lot of workers and their cause would seem to take priority. The boycott needs wide support to be effective. You'll support it, hope the Conlons can weather a temporary loss of business and try to help them in some other way.

You hate to see the Conlons' business damaged, but the farmers are employing illegal labor, and their produce deserves to be boycotted to bring pressure on them to obey the law. You'll support the boycott and hope it won't be necessary for it to last very long.

ASSESSMENT OF OPTIONS A. Stage Three B. Stage Two C. Stage Five D. Stage Four

The Housing Office

Suppose you are Ruth, a college senior on a large California campus. You've been a crusader, one of the leaders in student government. Among other things, you have led a demonstration for more student housing, and you were involved in setting up a student-run housing cooperative trying to assure fair living space for everybody.

You need a job to stay in school, and your friend Tom, whom you met in your work with the cooperative, is head of the University Housing Department. He hires you as his assistant.

As one of your duties, you are assigned to deal with students on the waiting list for the limited on-campus housing. Over and over, you must inform disappointed applicants that their names are far down the list and there are no immediate prospects for them. Since off-campus housing is scarce and prohibitively expensive, many students are forced to cancel their plans to attend the university.

As the spring semester is about to begin, Tom tells you to put two new applicants' names at the top of the list. You protest, saying it's unfair to the others who have waited so long. You've heard stories about this kind of thing but hadn't believed it really happened. Tom explains he's already made a strong objection, but the applicants are the son of a powerful alumnus and the son's friend, and the chancellor himself has ordered that preference be given them. Reluctantly you comply with Tom's order.

While routinely sorting material for the housing file that afternoon, you discover the vice-chancellor's confidential memo instructing Tom to "suspend regular procedures as a favor to this important friend of the university." A local reporter, interested in printing an expose of political favoritism involving the university, calls the office to check some rumors he's heard about the housing department. You take the call.

Angry over the injustice of the situation, you've made a pho-
tostatic copy of the chancellor's memo, and you are strongly
tempted to give it to the reporter. But, because of your friendship for Tom and your concern about your own job, which
you really need, you hesitate. You tell the reporter to leave his
number and you'll call him in a day or so if you have any information for him.

◆TIONAL ENDINGS

You really can't risk losing your job—you have to have it to
complete your senior year—it would be hard to find another
as good. You decide not to call the reporter.

You decide that, even though you hate to lose your job, which
will probably happen, and hate to harm Tom in any way, this
kind of thing is against all the rules and policies of the university and shouldn't be permitted. You give the memo to the reporter.

You make up your mind you can't sit by while an injustice
like this takes place; you've worked hard on the problems of
student housing and if you expose this kind of action it should
make things better for all the students in the future. Every
student deserves the same chance at housing as every other.
You'll give the reporter the memo and risk the loss of your
job.

Unhappy as you are over the unfairness of the situation, you
decide your first loyalty is to Tom, who is a decent guy, who
gave you the job, and who is doing everything possible to protest this kind of favoritism. If you release the memo, you could
get him in serious trouble. You decide not to call the reporter.

ASSESSMENT OF OPTIONS A. Stage Two B. Stage Four C.
Stage Five D. Stage Three

The Parking Lot

Suppose you are Alex Foster and have walked out of a supermarket to see a crowd of people gathered around your new red Camaro and a deep dent along the side of the car.

"Is this yours?" someone asks.

"I'm afraid so," you answer, dismayed.

"Well, don't worry. Lots of us here saw it and got the license number of the girl who hit you. It was an old blue VW. Here you go."

You take the proffered note with the number written on it and thank the woman. Other people in the crowd express sympathy and urge you to call the police right away.

Across town, Mary Rose, 16, is explaining to her mother why the right front fender of her car is so badly bent and has red paint marks on it. Mary says she was parked at the supermarket and found the fender that way when she came back to her car.

"I'm going right down there!" Mrs. Rose announces.

"Oh, no! Whoever did it must be gone by now. It'd be silly. Please don't," begs Mary. Ignoring Mary's pleas, her mother strides out to her own car.

You call the police, and the officer does a registration check. Someone will be sent to the address of the registered owner of the VW to investigate.

You hesitate and say, "I don't know. I don't want to make a big thing out of it."

"It won't take long," says the policeman. "You want your car repaired, don't you?"

"Well, yes, of course."

Mrs. Rose drives into the parking lot and immediately spots the red Camaro with the dent. "I'm glad you're here," she tells the police officer. "That man must be the one who hit my daughter's VW."

You interrupt. "Does she have a blue one with a license 225-RDL?"

Almost immediately a squad car pulls up with a tearful Mary in the back seat. Everyone starts talking at once. Mrs. Rose finally realizes that Mary, not you, is the offender, and begins to shout at her daughter. As the mother is calmed by one of the policemen, Mary, crying, tells you she's terribly sorry. She just got her driver's license and her "new" automobile; she was so excited that when she was parking and the clutch slipped a little she slid into your car. Afraid that her mother might take the VW away from her, she panicked and drove off. She had saved her allowance and all the money she could earn for a whole year to buy her little blue "bug."

The officer in charge says you have a choice: You can report the accident as a hit and run or merely turn it in as a standard claim with Mary's insurance company. Since there was no bodily injury and no damage over $500, the law doesn't require a police report but they will file one if you request it. Should you choose to file hit-and-run charges the case will be turned over to the district attorney. For misdemeanor hit and run, Mary could be fined, lose her license for a year or more, possibly have her insurance canceled.

You consider. Has Mary learned enough of a lesson, or does she need a stiff sentence to make her a more responsible driver? She seems genuinely remorseful. The mother is now meek as a lamb and offers to pay for whatever damage the insurance doesn't cover.

TIONAL ENDINGS

You feel sorry for Mary and believe her remorse is genuine. You feel she's young and has been punished enough. You hate to be the one to send her to the district attorney's office.

You decide that Mary broke the law and the only right thing to do is to hold her legally accountable; hit and run is a serious matter, and you decide to press charges.

Since Mary hit your car and tried to get out of her responsibility for the damage, she should pay for what she did. You decide to press charges. If she gets punished, it's only what she deserves.

D. You decide that, even though you're sorry for Mary, she's demonstrated incompetence and irresponsibility and isn't a very safe driver. Therefore charges should be brought against her to help her learn responsibility.

ASSESSMENT OF OPTIONS A. Stage Three B. Stage Four C. Stage One D. Stage Five

Rights

Suppose you are Austin Reeves, principal of a high school in Columbus County. You receive an anonymous phone call one day informing you that your school's respected English teacher, Bill Morley, has been seen in a nearby city marching in a parade supporting rights for homosexuals. State law stipulates that any teacher who engages in homosexual acts or who advocates homosexuality can be dismissed from his job.

You call Bill into your office to ask him about the incident and discover that Bill not only participated in the parade but readily admits to you he is a practicing homosexual. Bill says he sees no reason to make his sexual preference public, however, because he believes it has no relevance to his ability as a teacher.

A group of parents calls on you to tell you they have learned about Bill's participation in the parade. They say if you don't fire Bill they'll go to the school board and protest. When they leave, the spokeswoman says Bill's going to lose his job anyway—"And if you try to protect him, you'll lose yours too."

Bill is not only an excellent teacher, he's also a close friend and helped your family get established when you moved to Columbus County last year. Relatively new in the community, you don't yet have the wide support you need in a difficult situation like this. You believe it's quite possible you might lose your job if you try to defend Bill. You have three children. The job is a good one, and jobs aren't easy to find in your field. Should you risk it by supporting Bill, or should you fire him, as you legally can?

OPTIONAL ENDINGS

.. Bill has violated state law, and you feel you don't have much choice but to fire him. You're not there to interpret the law but to obey it.

B. You decide not to fire Bill but to defend him, because you consider the law against homosexual teachers unjust. Bill is a highly qualified teacher, much admired by the students, and there have been no complaints of any kind against him before.

C. You decide to defend Bill's right to march in the parade, even though your own job could be in jeopardy under the same law that now threatens Bill. You believe Bill's right to teach is worth the risk to your own position.

D. You decide to defend Bill because he's your colleague and friend and he's been helpful to you in many ways.

E. You make up your mind to fire Bill because your primary responsibility is to be a good principal and run a good school. This problem could create tremendous dissension in the community and among the parents, which would be very disruptive to your school.

ASSESSMENT OF OPTIONS A. Stage Four B. Stage Five C. Stage Five D. Stage Three E. Stage Three

The Leukemia Dilemma
(As reported in the *Boston Globe,* March 3, 1978)

Massachusetts General Hospital (MGH) officials decided last night to fight a Brockton probate judge's ruling that two-year-old Chad Green be returned to the legal custody of his parents, who plan to discontinue conventional medical treatment for his leukemia and seek unorthodox "dietary" therapy.

Plymouth County Probate Judge James Lawton ruled yesterday morning that Gerald and Diane Green of Scituate are "not unfit" to retain custody of Chad merely because they wish to abandon the conventional chemotherapy that medical experts say is the child's only hope of survival.

MGH spokesman Martin Bander said yesterday evening that hospital officials feel "morally obligated" to pursue other legal avenues to ensure Chad's continued treatment. "To stop treatment now," Bander said in a prepared statement, "would be not only to abandon Chad but also in a sense to abandon thousands of future Chads whose parents unwittingly wish to condemn their children to a painful death—children too young to decide for themselves."

The boy's father said after the Brockton hearing that he and his wife would fight further attempts by the hospital to continue chemotherapy.

The MGH's decision to pursue its legal battle makes it likely that Chad's case will become a landmark confrontation between established medical opinion and adherents of unorthodox cancer therapies as well as a test of who should decide about the treatment of a minor.

Dr. John T. Truman of the MGH, who has managed the boy's care, said yesterday, "If treatment is discontinued at this point, it can be said with 100 percent confidence that the disease will recur and he will die within a period of one to six months." With treatment, Truman said, his chances of survival are less than 50 percent but still substantial.

Diane Green said after the hearing, "For my husband and me, quality of life is more important than quantity. We would rather see Chad have a short, wonderful life as himself than to have a life extended by poisonous drugs and needles."

Truman said that the two-year-old, who is at home with his parents, has so far suffered "minimal side effects" from the anticancer drugs he took last fall and again this month. The Greens, who moved to Boston from Nebraska to find the best available treatment for their son, contradicted Truman, saying that the therapy has terrified the child and has been physically and emotionally exhausting.

"Have you ever seen a child turn into a mad dog?" the father said. "That's what our child does because of the poisons they have been giving him. . . . There has to be a better way than to poison the human system in order to cure it."

Last November, the Greens discontinued Chad's chemotherapy without informing the doctors, substituting a regimen of organic foods, vitamins, and distilled water. Though the boy had been in remission, he suffered a recurrence of his blood cancer in February, when the Greens admitted they had stopped the prescribed treatment.

In ruling in favor of the parents' motion to regain legal control over their son, Judge Lawton agreed with the recommendation of Chad's temporary guardian, Attorney John H. Wyman of Plymouth, who was appointed by the court to represent the boy's best interests.

Wyman told the judge that the parents' decision to forego further chemotherapy is "a rational parental decision, perhaps one that I might not personally make, but one that I can respect."

Without taking further testimony from doctors or from parents of children who have been successfully treated for leukemia, Lawton announced that "there is no way we are going to be able to establish that the parents of Chad Green are unfit. I am satisfied that they are not."

This true story is used as a teaching dilemma, one of those presented in *Moral Education,* a classroom workbook by Thomas and Muriel Ladenburg and Peter Scharf.

Since their book was published, another chapter has been added to the story. As indicated in the *Boston Globe* account, the hospital officials did pursue the matter further in the courts. Superior Court Judge Guy Volterra, in a 46-page opinion, said, "If treated, this child will run, play, and go to school. Untreated, he will lapse into pain and death. The agony of death from leukemia is far more painful to this minor than the minimal side effects and pinpricks caused by chemotherapy." Judge Volterra ordered the boy's treatment continued at Massachusetts General Hospital and said he saw no evidence of side effects. He held that the parents' fear of chemotherapy "is not supported by the evidence of the case."

Under interim court order, the Greens had been taking Chad almost daily to the hospital for chemotherapy. The ruling left Chad in his parents' custody but made the state department of public welfare his legal guardian to ensure that they complied with the Judge's order.

After Judge Volterra's decision, the Greens left their home in Massachusetts and flew Chad to a laetrile clinic in Tijuana, Mexico, to continue the treatment they felt was best for him. The Massachusetts Appeals Court upheld Judge Volterra's finding and ordered the Greens not to give their son laetrile therapy.

Would you side with Judge Lawton or with Judge Volterra? Do parents have the right to decide what is best for their child, even if it is contrary to the consensus of expert medical opinion?

ASSESSMENT OF OPTIONS

The argument that parents have the right to treat Chad as they wish because he is their child is indicative of Stage Two reasoning—people may do whatever they wish with what belongs to them.

Reasoning on the basis of whether the doctors or the parents have the best interests of the child at heart would be a Stage Three concept, dealing with interpersonal relationships and care for others.

At Stage Four, the important factors are the legal concepts—whether the child's or the parent's legal rights are being violated.

A Stage Five approach would consider the prospects for Chad's recovery under both types of treatment, weighing the harm done to him by chemotherapy against his chances for cure or remission with unorthodox methods.

Judge Lawton believed the parents had their child's best interests at heart and had the right to accept or reject the treatment proposed. This is primarily a Stage Three concept.

Judge Volterra weighed the evidence for both kinds of therapy and was convinced that Chad would die without the chemotherapy. Seeing Chad's life as the most important issue, he ordered the treatment continued. This would fit more closely with Stage Five reasoning.

The Apartment

Suppose you are Milly. You and Harold live in the same rather shabby apartment complex, and both of you are retired. Harold is 75, and you admit to 70. Although Harold worked hard to put away a nest egg for his old age and has a small pension from the company where he worked for 25 years, it's difficult to meet even the basic expenses of living the way inflation is driving up prices. You live on your widow's social security benefits, which barely enable you to get along from month to month. Both you and Harold have grown children, but none of them have enough extra space to take in a parent. Besides, you'd prefer to be independent. You're a devout Baptist, supervise the nursery at the church every Sunday morning, and have been a dedicated churchgoer all of your life.

You and Harold have become friends, sharing interests, helping each other endure the pressures and the loneliness of your lifestyle. On occasion you get together in your tiny efficiency apartment for dinner, or go to the special dollar matinee at the neighborhood movie house, or join the church square-dancing parties.

The owner of your building mails a notice of an immediate 20 percent rent increase. This means both you and Harold will have to move, probably to an even more run-down neighborhood. Harold says that's terrible enough, but the possibility of losing his friendship with you is even worse.

You're equally disturbed at the prospect of your separation. Close to tears, you tell Harold, "Maybe I'll just move into a retirement home. I've read there are places that will take care of you if you sign over your social security checks to them."

"Those places are awful," Harold says. "You'd hate it."

"I know," you tell him. "But there aren't many choices left for us."

Harold's anger increases as he considers the indignity of your predicament. "Let's fight! Let's do something!"

You have to smile at that. "I'd love to fight. But what can we do?"

"You move in with me, and we'll cut our rent and our utilities in half."

You're shocked. "Oh, Harold!"

"Why not? It's a nice, clean place. We'd cut down on our food bills, too."

"Getting married at our age?" You stare down at your shoes.

"Oh, we wouldn't get married. Couldn't. Our social security would be cut back if they found out. Then we'd be no better off than we are now."

You are silent. This goes against your deepest moral convictions. Living with a man without marrying him? What would your children say? How could you face your friends? And wouldn't this be cheating the social security? You aren't quite sure about that point but the whole arrangement violates everything you've always believed in.

OPTIONAL ENDINGS

A. Since you so desperately need a reasonably priced place to live and cherish your friendship with Harold, you believe in this way you could help yourselves and be less of a burden to your children and to society. You take a deep breath and tell Harold you'll live with him.

B. Your whole concept of right conduct, doing the proper thing, tells you you shouldn't take this step. Using the money from your husband's social security earnings to live intimately with a man without marrying him is no way for a decent woman to behave. You reluctantly say no and hope Harold will come to see you in the retirement home when you locate one.

C. Even though you find it hard to accept such an informal living arrangement, your basic need is for a reasonable and decent home and good companionship. You decide Harold's idea is a practical arrangement that will benefit both of you.

You're torn by your affection and need for Harold, your love for your children, and your need for their approval and that of your friends. After a lot of soul searching, you decide your feeling for Harold is the strongest pull and you'll move into his apartment.

You believe that marriage and the family are the most important things in anyone's life. If you lived with Harold, you'd be going against the customs, morals, and rules you've believed in all of your life. You opt for the retirement home.

ASSESSMENT OF OPTIONS A. Stage Five B. Stage Three C. Stage Two D. Stage Three E. Stage Four

Donovan's Disco

Suppose you are Fred, a high-school senior doing a little shopping with your friend Peter. You are browsing through Donovan's Disco, a vast establishment with rows of tables filled with records and tapes, hard rock pounding from speakers around the room. Both of you are carrying backpacks filled with school books. Peter spots a special tape of the Bee-Gees—it's $12.95, and he only has about $7 with him. When he asks you to loan him the money, you tell him you're really sorry but you only have $5 with you. Anyway, it's money you've been saving for an album you really crave—Crab Grass' latest LP. You stoop down to look under a counter to see if there are any other Crab Grass titles on the lower shelf. Just as you stand up, you see Peter slip the BeeGees tape into his back pack. You open your mouth, but before you can say anything Peter cuts you off: "Gotta split. I'll call you tonight."

You're still standing in amazement when the store manager approaches and asks you to step into the office. The manager tells you one of the clerks is sure he saw Peter pick up a tape, but before he could catch up with him Peter had disappeared. The clerk says he's pretty sure you and Peter came in together. The manager asks you who Peter is and where he lives. "We'll find him anyway, but if you can help us it'll save a lot of trouble. We'll give you a free single."

You shake your head. You don't want a free single. You have the money—you just want to buy that Crab Grass album. The manager persists. If you helped Peter steal the tape, you're an accomplice. The police might want to talk to you. What about it?

PTIONAL ENDINGS

A. You tell the manager you just happened to be standing with Peter in the store and you don't know his last name or where he lives. You might need a favor from Peter some day—it's not your business to be responsible for what Peter does.

B. You deny you know Peter, because he's your friend and you don't rat on a friend. You'd feel terrible if the guys at school heard you'd turned Peter in and gotten him in trouble.

C. You're a little nervous and don't want to be involved with the police, so you decide to tell the manager Peter's name and address. Stealing is wrong, it's against the law, and if you're going to steal you should expect to be punished.

D. You tell the manager Peter's name because you don't believe anyone has a right to steal, to take what doesn't belong to him. The world would be in a mess if everybody did things like that.

ASSESSMENT OF OPTIONS A. Stage Two B. Stage Three C. Stage One D. Stage Four

The Family

Suppose you are Betty Edwards, mother of a middle-class family living in Chicago. Dave Edwards, the father, has recently been committed to a mental institution. You have been left with the responsibility for yourself and four children—aged two, three, five, and eight. You've had to sell your house to meet your debts and are living temporarily in a friend's small apartment. There's a housing shortage, and you're having problems finding another place.

The medical assessment of Dave's condition is that his illness is serious, and it will probably take some time for him to recover. According to the doctor, Dave has a better chance if he gets support and affection from you and the children, and he encourages you to visit as often as you can.

You get depressed when you go to see Dave in the pale green wards on the third floor. You still love him, still remember so many good years, but this Dave is different from the man you have lived with for such a long time. You resent his seeming lack of concern about your problems and his indifference to the children's welfare. You have to remind yourself that this isn't the real Dave—his thinking is temporarily distorted.

The company where Dave worked has a limited disability plan, and the money is about to run out. Your parents live in a roomy old house in Florida large enough for you and the children; the older couple could help look after the children while you try to find a job. It won't be easy. You haven't many skills, and you haven't worked except for six months just before you married Dave. And, even though your parents are cooperative, they are elderly and couldn't handle four young children by themselves. You would have to go to Florida with them.

When you tell Dave you feel the move is the only way to keep the family afloat financially, he cries like a child and begs you not to go.

You're torn—uncertain how you can manage if you try to stay in Chicago; hesitant about leaving the children during the day without proper supervision even if you're able to find a job. You wouldn't be able to afford a real housekeeper but would have to get along with teenage babysitters or help from the neighbors. Yet you hate to leave Dave. You think it's possible his recovery may indeed depend on regular and supportive visits from you and the children.

OPTIONAL ENDINGS

A. You're torn between your love and concern for your husband and your love and concern for the children. You know it will be better for Dave if you stay in Chicago, but you're equally sure it will be better for the children if you move to Florida, at least until Dave gets well. You decide to go. You'll write often, and if you get a good job you can afford to fly back to visit him occasionally.

B. You are concerned about the family's financial situation, which is desperate. There's no question it would be a good move, from that standpoint, to move to Florida where you'd have free rent, free and responsible help with the children, and a chance for you to earn and save some money to get the family back on its feet again.

C. You decide your obligation is to Dave and the children equally, and the important thing is to keep the family together. You decide to stay in Chicago, make the best arrangement you can for the children, and find some kind of job—or to swallow your pride and seek welfare help if necessary. The marriage contract is the important one, and you have a responsibility to keep it going and help Dave recover.

ASSESSMENT OF OPTIONS A. Stage Three. B. Stage Two C. Stage Five

One for the Road

Suppose you are Carole Griffin. You know your husband, Gordon, has been having an affair with a young woman in his office. He's been almost flagrant about it, but, after some serious quarrels and a warning from you that all this is leading to a break-up of your marriage, he has promised to stop seeing the girl outside the office. You have two children, aged 7 and 12, and you desperately want to keep the family together and rebuild your strained relationship with your husband.

One morning Gordon tells you he's going directly from the office to the airport that evening. He has to be in Seattle for an early meeting and feels it's safer to leave the night before. Both cities are having cab strikes, and he can't risk any last-minute complications—it's important that he be on time.

That night you find a piece of paper on the floor next to Gordon's desk, confirming an early morning plane reservation to Seattle for the following day. When your friend Nancy drops by the house, she discovers you in tears. Hearing the story, Nancy suggests you both drive down to the girl friend's apartment to see whether Gordon's car is there. You protest—what will that accomplish? Anyway, he's too prudent to park his car near the building. Nancy says, "How do you know? Come on. This is a perfect chance to find out if he's keeping his promise to you."

You drive to the girl's apartment; by now it's close to midnight. There sits Gordon's long brown Oldsmobile, silent confirmation of Carole's fears. Nancy stares at the car and says suddenly: "That bastard! I'm going to let the air out of his tires."

Carole, who has been slumped down in the seat, hurt, abject, despairing, starts to laugh.

"Nancy, you're wonderful! You wouldn't really do that!"
"Oh, yes, I would,"
"But what if he catches you?"
"So what if he catches me? He deserves it, the creep. Be-

sides, he's tucked in all safe and snug with his playmate. He's not going anywhere tonight. You saw the note about his flight tomorrow morning."

"But if you give him four flat tires he'll probably miss the plane—he might even miss his meeting. That won't help his situation at the office—his job's kind of precarious as it is."

Ignoring all of this, Nancy hops out, gets a screwdriver from the glove compartment, and starts busily working on a valve stem. Carole sits in the car, wavering. She doesn't really want to hurt Gordon's career—losing his job won't help repair their faltering marriage. Or will it? At least he wouldn't be working with that girl every day. And Carole can't help enjoying the fact that this is the first time since Gordon's affair began that somebody in her corner has done anything except sympathize, weep, or wring their hands. A bit nervous, Carole keeps glancing at the entrance door of the apartment building. Everything is quiet except for the hissing sound as Nancy releases the air and Gordon's car slowly settles lower and lower.

Now that you're familiar with the way different levels of reasoning can be used to solve moral dilemmas, you can choose several ways of looking at this situation, with your own estimate of what stage of moral development each one would indicate.

For example, if you were Carole, would you try to stop Nancy, protecting Gordon from the possibility of missing his meeting and jeopardizing his job? That could indicate a Stage Three concern with relationships, with doing what a good wife should do, even when she's feeling betrayed. Or would you do as the woman in this story actually did—sit laughing helplessly, thinking of her husband' s face the next morning, and about how he had been deliberately letting the life out of their once-joyous marriage just like her friend releasing the air from his tires? This eye for an eye concept is identified as Stage One in Kohlberg's writings; or it might be seen as a kind of negative reciprocity typical of Stage Two. What seems right from your viewpoint?

How Would You Solve
These Dilemmas?

Following are some mini-dilemmas to give *you* an opportunity to create your own options and decide where you think they fit on the levels of moral reasoning.

You are a married woman and have three children. Because your husband has developed a serious heart condition and is unable to work, you've taken a job to support the family. There's terrific pressure on you because of the family's current financial needs and a pile of past-due bills. Your boss offers to double your salary if you'll agree to a more intimate relationship. He also implies you might lose your job unless you go along with his suggestion. It's a good, high-paying position, and you know you'll have a hard time getting another like it. He's an attractive, discreet man—no one will know about the situation unless you yourself choose to disclose it. What would you do?

You're a doctor. You deliver a baby with both arms and legs missing and indications of other abnormalities. Since the child is not strong, special measures will probably be needed to keep it alive. You have taken an oath as a physician to protect and prolong life. What would you do?

You've been saving to buy a ring for your fiancee and still don't have enough. A friend offers you one from a dubious source—you have it appraised, and the price your friend has quoted is about a third of the real value of the ring. Would you buy it?

You find a $500 error in your bank account, in your favor. Would you call it to the bank's attention? Immediately? Wait for them to discover it?

You're on the committee for a ball to raise funds for a hospital that treats crippled children who might otherwise be unable to receive the necessary medical and surgical care. The guests at the party buy chips with which to gamble, and the more the house wins, the more funds go to the hospital. You're running the roulette wheel, and you've accidentally found a way to rig it in your favor. The players are wealthy people who can well afford to lose. What would you do?

Your house has been robbed, and you've lost many valuable items. As you're making up a list for the insurance company, a friend drops by. He says you should inflate the value of the items because insurance companies make huge profits and also they will undoubtedly depreciate the amount of the loss you claim. What would you do?

You're filling out an application for an important job you want very much. You aren't really fully qualified in one of the areas they ask you about, but you're sure you can handle the job and can soon master all the aspects of it. Would you touch up your record a little to make it look better than it really is?

Bibliography

Amnesty International, *Report on Torture*. New York: Farrar, Strauss & Giroux, 1975.

"An Amnesty Group at Work." *Matchbox* (Amnesty International newsletter), Winter, 1977, p. 9.

Arendt, H. *Eichmann in Jerusalem*. New York: Viking, 1963.

Beard, R. *Piaget's Developmental Psychology*. New York: New American Library, 1969.

Blatt, M., Colby, A., and Speicher, B. "Hypothetical Dilemmas for Use in Moral Discussions." Cambridge, Mass.: Harvard University, Moral Education and Research Foundation, 1974.

Blatt, M., and Kohlbert, L. "The Effects of Classroom Moral Discussion upon Children's Level of Moral Judgment." Unpublished doctoral dissertation, University of Chicago, 1968.

Bok, S. *Lying: Moral Choice in Public and Private Life*. New York; Pantheon Books, 1978.

Brenner, S. and Molander, E. "Is The Ethics of Business Changing?" *Harvard Business Review*, 1977, *55*, 47.

Book review. *Time* 111, no. 14 (April 3, 1978): 67.

Brinton, H. H. *Friends for Three Hundred Years*. Wallingford, Pa.: Pendle Hill, 1965.

Cahn, S. "Justice Black and First Amendment 'Absolutes': A Public Interview." *New York University Law Review*, 37, 1962: 549–557.

Campbell, S. F., *Piaget: A Sampler* New York: Wiley, 1976.

Candee, D. "The Moral Psychology of Watergate." *Journal of Social Issues*, 1975, *31*, (2), 183–192.

Christian, J. L. *Philosophy: An Introduction to the Art of Wondering*. New York: Holt, Rinehart and Winston, 1973.

Cope, O. *The Breast, Its Problems, Benign and Malignant*. Boston; Houghton Mifflin, 1972.

Cimons, M. "A Vision of Peace from Ulster." *Los Angeles Times*, 26 March 1978, part IV, pp. 1, 15.

Dewey, J. *Democracy and Education*. New York: Free Press, 1916.

Dewey, J. "What Psychology Can Do for the Teacher." (1895). In Archambault (Ed.) *John Dewey On Education*. New York: Modern Library, 1963.

Dewey, J., and Tufts, J. *Ethics*. New York: Holt, Rinehart and Winston, 1932.

Dewey, J. *Human Nature and Conduct*. New York: Modern Library, 1930.

Dimont, M. I., *Jews, God and History*. New York: Simon & Schuster, 1962.

Durant, W. *The Story of Philosophy*. New York: Simon & Schuster, 1926.

BIBLIOGRAPHY

uska, R., and Whelan, M. *Moral Development.* New York: Paulist Press, 1975.

nerson, R. W. "Self-Reliance." in *Essays of Ralph Waldo Emerson.* (1841) New York: Thomas Y. Crowell, 1926.

·dynast, A. "Improving the Adequacy of Moral Reasoning." Unpublished doctoral dissertation, Harvard University Graduate School of Business Administration, 1973.

aenkel, J. "The Kohlberg Bandwagon: Some Reservations." *Social Education,* 1976, *40* (4), 216–222.

ankema, W. K. *Ethics.* Englewood Cliffs, N.J.: Prentice-Hall, 1963.

·omm, E. *Man for Himself.* New York: Holt, Rinehart and Winston, 1960.

albraith, R. E., and Jones, T. M. *Moral Reasoning.* Anoka, Minn: Greenhaven Press, 1976.

illigan, C. "In a Different Voice." *Harvard Educational Review,* 1977, *47* (4), 481–517.

oldman, J. "Halls of Heroes Forgotten in Celebrity Age." *Los Angeles Times,* 24 May 1978, pp. 1, 8, 9.

ood *Housekeeping* 185, no. 4 (October, 1977): 245–262.

all, E. "A Conversation With Jean Piaget and Barbel Inhelder." In *Readings in Psychology Today,* Del Mar, Calif. CRM Books, 1967.

artshorne, H., and May, M. A. *Studies in the Nature of Character.* New York: Macmillan, 1928–1930.

eilbroner, R. L. *The Human Prospect.* New York: Norton, 1974.

eller, J. *Catch 22,* New York: Dell, 1955.

ill, I. *The Ethical Basis of Economic Freedom.* Chapel Hill, N.Y.: American Viewpoint, 1976.

offer, E. *The True Believer.* New York: Harper & Row, 1951.

Horn, J. "The Third Wave: Nazism in a High School." *Psychology Today,* 1976, *10* (2), 14–17.

Hunt, R., and Arras, J. *Ethical Issues in Modern Medicine.* Palo Alto, Calif.; Mayfield Publishing, 1977.

Illich, I. *Celebration of Awareness.* New York: Doubleday, 1969.

Illich, I. *Medical Nemesis.* New York: Random House, 1976.

"Insanity Defense Pleas Called Charade." *Los Angeles Times,* 9 June 1978, part I, p. 14.

"It's Not Only West Point That Has Cheating Problems." *U. S. News and World Report* 80, no. 24 (June 14, 1976): 35–36.

Joy, C. R. *Albert Schweitzer: An Anthology.* Boston: Beacon Press, 1947.

King, M. L. *Why We Can't Wait.* New York: Harper & Row, 1963.

Kavanaugh, J. *The Quaker Approach.* New York: Putnam's, 1953.

Kohlberg, L. "A Cognitive Developmental Analysis of Children's Sex-Role Concepts and Attitudes." In E. E. Maccoby (ed.), *The Development of Sex Differences,* Stanford, Calif.: Stanford University Press, 1966.

Kohlberg, L. "The Child as a Moral Philosopher." *Psychology Today,* 1968, *1,* 25–30.

Kohlberg, L. "Stage and Sequence: The Cognitive Developmental Approach to Socialization." In D. A. Goslin (ed.), *Handbook of Socialization Theory and Research.* New York: Rand McNally, 1969.

Kohlberg, L. "The Concepts of Developmental Psychology as the Central Guide to Education: Examples from Cognitive, Moral, and Psychological Education. In Maynard C. Reynolds (ed.), *The Proceedings of the Conference on Psychology and the Process of*

Schooling in the Next Decade. Minneapolis, Minn.: Alternative Conceptions, University of Minnesota, 1971a.

Kohlberg, L. "From Is to Ought; How to Commit the Naturalistic Fallacy and Get Away With It." In T. Mischel (ed.), *Cognitive Development and Epistemology.* New York: Academic Press, 1971.

Kohlberg, L. "The Claim to Moral Adequacy of a Highest Stage of Moral Judgment." In L. Kohlberg and E. Turiel (eds.), *Moralization: The Cognitive Developmental Approach.* New York: Holt, Rinehart and Winston, 1973a.

Kohlberg, L. "Continuities in Childhood and Adult Moral Development Revisited." In L. Kohlberg and E. Turiel (eds.), *Moralization: the Cognitive Developmental Approach.* New York: Holt, Rinehart and Winston, 1973b.

Kohlberg, L. "Stages and Aging in Moral Development." *The Gerontologist,* 1973c, V. *13* (4) 497–502.

Kohlberg, L. "Education, Moral Development and Faith," *Journal of Moral Education,* 1974a, *4,* (5) 5–16.

Kohlberg, L. "Lessons of Watergate." American Psychological Association Comments, New Orleans, 1974b.

Kohlberg, L. "Beyond Psychology and Beyond Ethics—Spinoza's View." Unpublished paper, 1975a.

Kohlberg, L. "Children's Perceptions of Contemporary Value Systems." Unpublished paper, Harvard Interfaculty Seminar on Raising Children in Modern Urban America, 1975b.

Kohlberg, L. "The Cognitive Development Approach to Behavior Disorders: A Study of the Development of Moral Reasoning in Delinquents." Paper presented at Kittay Scientific Foundation Conference, April 1977.

Kohlberg, L. "The Future of Liberali as the Dominant Ideology of West." Unpublished paper.

Kohlberg, L. "The Domain and Dev opment of Moral Judgment." Adap from *Assessing Moral Judgm Stages,* in preparation.

Kohlberg, L. "Will the Supreme Co Recognize the Right to Dignity?" L published paper, 1975c.

Kohlberg, L., and Boyd, D. "Politi and Moral Choice and the Problem Civil Disobedience." Unpublished per, 1975.

Kohlberg, L., and Elfenbein, D. "T Development of Moral Judgme Concerning Capital Punishmen *American Journal of Orthopsychiat* 1975, *45* (4), 614–640.

Kohlberg, L., and Gilligan, C. "T Adolescent as a Philosopher: The D covery of the Self in a Postconve tional World." *Daedalus: Journal the American Academy of Arts a Sciences,* 1971, *100* (4), 1051–1086.

Kohlberg, L., and Mayer, R. "Develo ment as the Aim of Education." *Ha vard Educational Review,* 1972, (4), 449–496.

Kohlberg, L., and Scharf, P. "Burea cratic Violence and Convention Moral Thinking." *The Americc Journal of Orthopsychiatry,* 1972, 16.

Kohlberg, L., and Tapp, J. L. "Deve oping Senses of Law and Legal Ju tice." *Journal of Social* Issues, 197 *27* (2), 65–91.

Kohlberg, L., and Turiel, E. "Mor Development and Moral Education In G. Lesser (ed.), *Psychology and t Education Process.* Glenview, Il Scott, Foresman, 1971.

Kohlberg, L., Rest, J., and Turiel, "Relations Between the Level of Mo

BIBLIOGRAPHY

Judgment and Preference and Comprehension of Moral Judgment of Others." *Journal of Personality,* 1969.

lberg, L., Kauffman, K , Scharf, P., nd Hickey, J. "The Just Community Approach to Corrections." Camridge, Mass.: Harvard University, Moral Education Research Foundaon, 1974.

bs, R., and Kohlberg, L. "Moral Judgment and Ego Controls as Deterninants of Resistance to Cheating." n L. Kohlberg and E. Turiel (eds.), *Moralization: The Cognitive Developnental Approach.* New York: Holt, Rinehart and Winston, 1973.

lenburg, T., Ladenburg, M., and Scharf, P. *Moral Education: A Classoom Workbook.* Davis, Calif.: Reponsible Action, 1978.

opold, A. *Sand County Almanac.* New York: Oxford University Press, 1949.

ooking for a Reason." *Time* 110, no. 4 July 25, 1977): 17.

cDougall, W. *An Introduction to Social Psychology.* London: Methuen, 1908.

Williams, C. *Factories in the Field.* Santa Barbara, Calif: Peregrine Press, 1971.

lgram, S. "Behavioral Study of Obedience," *Journal of Abnormal and Social Psychology,* 1963, *67,* 371–378.

ll, J. S. *On Liberty.* Indianapolis, Ind.: Bobbs-Merrill, 1956. (Originally published 1859.)

iller, M. *Plain Speaking.* New York: Putnam's, 1973.

iller, W. R. *Martin Luther King, Jr.* New York: Weybright & Talley, 1968.

uir, W. K., Jr., *Police: Streetcorner Politicians.* Chicago: University of Chicago, 1977.

ary, J. "Where Have All The Heroes Gone?" *Saturday Review,* 1976, *3* (16), 10–11.

North, R. C., *The World That Could Be.* Stanford, Calif: Stanford Alumni Association, 1976.

Oswald, R. L. *Lee: A Portrait.* New York: Coward, McCann & Geoghegan, 1967.

"Our Children Don't Know How to Play." *Los Angeles Times,* 11 Oct. 1977, part I, p. 6.

Pagliuoso, S. *Understanding Stages of Moral Development (Workbook).* New York: Paulist Press, 1976.

Peck, R. F., and Havighurst, R. J. *The Psychology of Character Development.* New York: Wiley, 1960.

Piaget, J. *The Moral Judgment of the Child.* New York: Free Press, 1965.

Piaget, J. *To Understand Is to Invent.* New York: Viking, 1974.

"Police Probing Reports by Ex-Residents of Synanon." *Los Angeles Times,* 31 October 1978, part I, pp. 1, 23.

Redd, R. "A Rebel Priest's Hope for Ireland." *US,* March 21, 1978, pp. 32–33.

Riesman, D. *The Lonely Crowd.* New Haven, Conn.: Yale University Press, 1961.

Rosenblatt, R. A. "President Not Given Data by Aides." *Los Angeles Times* 13 Sept. 1977, pp. 1, 6.

"The Saints Among Us." *Time* 106, no. 26 (December 29, 1975): 47–56.

Sampson, A. *The Sovereign State of ITT.* New York: Stein and Day, 1973.

Scharf, P *Moral Education.* Davis, Calif.: Responsible Action, 1978.

Schulberg, B. *What Makes Sammy Run?* New York: Penguin, 1978.

Seligman, J. "The Trust Treatment." *Newsweek* 89, no. 7 (February 14, 1977): 78.

Sheehan, S. *A Prison and a Prisoner.* New York: Houghton Mifflin, 1978.

Sinclair, U. *The Jungle.* New York: Lancer Books, 1970.

Smith, L. *Killers of the Dream.* New York: Norton, 1949.

Sorrentino, J. *The Moral Revolution.* Los Angeles: Nash, 1972.

Strick, A. *Injustice for All.* New York: Putnam's, 1977.

Szent-Gyorgyi, A. "On the Tragic Effects of Bureaucratic Interference in Basic Cancer Research." *Executive Health,* 1978.

Tabor, D., Paolitto, D., Isbel, S., Elfenbein, D. "A Report to the Staff of the Law in a Free Society Project." Unpublished report, 1976.

Taylor, R. B., *Sweatshops in the Sun.* Boston: Beacon Press, 1973.

Teilhard de Chardin, Pierre. *The Future of Man.* New York: Harper & Row, 1959.

Turnbull, C. *The Mountain Peop* New York: Simon and Schuster, 19

Ullmann, L. *Changing.* New Yo Knopf, 1977.

Wasserman, E. R. "Implementing Ko berg's Just Community Concept in Alternative High School." *Social E cation,* 1976, *40* (4), 216–222.

Wasserstrom, R. *Today's Moral Pr lems.* New York: Macmillan, 1975.

Weizmann, R., Brown, R., Levinson, and Taylor, P. (eds.), *Piagetian T ory and Its Implications for the Hel ing Professions.* Los Angeles: Univ sity of Southern California, 1978.

Woodward, K. L. "Moral Education *Newsweek* 87, no. 9 (March 1, 197 74–75.

Zimbardo. P. G. *Pathology of Impriso ment. Society,* 1972, *9,* (6), 4–8.